COMMUNICATION CONNECTION

Enrich Communication in your Marriage and Family

Ellen Dean

outskirts
press

COMMUNICATION CONNECTION
Enrich Communication in your Marriage and Family
All Rights Reserved.
Copyright © 2020 Ellen Dean
v3.0

The opinions expressed in this manuscript are solely the opinions of the author and do not represent the opinions or thoughts of the publisher. The author has represented and warranted full ownership and/or legal right to publish all the materials in this book.

This book may not be reproduced, transmitted, or stored in whole or in part by any means, including graphic, electronic, or mechanical without the express written consent of the publisher except in the case of brief quotations embodied in critical articles and reviews.

Outskirts Press, Inc.
http://www.outskirtspress.com

ISBN: 978-1-9772-3098-0

Cover Photo © 2020 www.gettyimages.com. All rights reserved - used with permission.

THE HOLY BIBLE, NEW INTERNATIONAL VERSION® NIV® Copyright(C) 1973, 1978, 1984, 2011 Biblica Inc.®
Used by permission. All rights reserved worldwide.

Outskirts Press and the "OP" logo are trademarks belonging to Outskirts Press, Inc.

PRINTED IN THE UNITED STATES OF AMERICA

ENDORSEMENTS

As a communicator and teacher of preaching, I have read many books on the subject of communication. *Communication Connection* without doubt is one of the best. This book covers all the key aspects of communication from a solidly biblical perspective. Ellen Dean is an experienced counselor and her book is practical and relevant. Her insights will enhance marriages, strengthen relationships, and resolve conflicts. This book is a true gem. Highly recommended!

Dr. David L. Allen
Distinguished Professor of Preaching
Southwestern Baptist Theological Seminary, Fort Worth, Texas

This book, *Communication Connection*, is desperately needed in today's culture. For years, the importance of communication in relationships has been noted by counselors, yet Ellen has gone one much-needed step further. She has addressed relational communication from a solidly biblical perspective in dealing with heart issues to arrive at practical principles which connect with readers. There is not a more comprehensive work on relational communication, that covers as many meaningful issues from a biblical perspective, viewed through the lens of a long-time, effective biblical counselor. Ellen knows relationship struggles and she knows the Scripture. I have recommended clients to her for more than fifteen years.

In Chapter 5, *Communication Connection* does an excellent job of describing words which build up rather than tear down relationships. The author weaves biblical concepts, such as affirmation, praise, appreciation, gentleness, and compassion, into case studies which allow readers to grasp them immediately. In Chapter 6, Ellen shows brilliantly how persons can connect during conflict. She suggests some of the best conflict guidelines I have read. Then, the book closes by poignantly showing how God demonstrated the most amazing communication ever in sending His Son, Jesus, to Earth.

I recommend *Communication Connection* to you unequivocally. Ellen Dean has masterfully constructed a guide to enrich communication in relationships, especially in marriage and families. Every individual and family can benefit from this book.

Dr. Greg Ammons, Senior Pastor
First Baptist Church, Garland, Texas

Ellen Dean has penned another most helpful and enlightening book on marriage. The reader will certainly receive great insights from the author's study of the Bible and from many years of her personal experiences as both a professional counselor and a pastor's wife. I heartily recommend this book to you.

Dr. Gary Cook, Chancellor
Dallas Baptist University Dallas, Texas

Most understand that spouses are expected to "leave and cleave" but not many know how this is supposed to look in real life. "Cleave" means "to pursue hard," which is fleshed out in this excerpt from the book:

"Spouses need to continually build their repertoire of common interests in life. Branch out to explore new activities, hobbies, areas of service and skills. Limited desire to pursue the relationship is a problem than can debilitate a marriage."

Communication Connection is full of practical encouragement like this which can be immediately applied. I wholeheartedly recommend it to anyone who is serious about growing their marriage.

Mark Dance, D.Min.
East Central Regional Ministry Partner
Baptist General Convention of Oklahoma

I have known and valued Ellen Dean, personally and professionally, for years. Her commitment to the application of God's word to real-life issues is unwavering, and in this new book on communication, God's word shines through. I commend Ellen's practical, biblical counsel on one of the great treasures God has given us—the blessing of communication.

Mark Farish Senior Pastor
Lake Highlands Baptist Church, Dallas, Texas

God designed marriage for the husband and wife to connect deeply and intimately, but failures in their communication will destroy that connection. My friend Ellen Dean wrote *Communication Connection* so that marriages can be saved, restored, and strengthened by learning biblical principles on how to communicate well and in a Christ-like manner.

Dr. Jack Graham, Senior Pastor,
Prestonwood Baptist Church, Dallas, Texas

Ellen Dean, with clarity, compassion, and competence, has written another book which provides an exceptional resource for strengthening the bonds of relationships. In this recent work, Ellen sets her sights on one of the most common challenges in any relationship—COMMUNICATION.

Communication Connection is well-organized and substantive. The reader will certainly appreciate the numerous scriptural references, helpful anecdotes, practical wisdom, and the graciously addressed issues in the quest to communicate effectively and properly in relationships. Especially helpful are the chapters offering insightful assistance in the manner of "tools and techniques" and "frequently asked questions." I have known Ellen Dean for more than two decades and she has consistently modeled the principles articulated in her book, both personally and professionally. I highly commend this resource to anyone seeking to improve their own Communication Connection!

Dr. John Hall, Senior Pastor
Field Street Baptist Church, Cleburne, Texas

I am thrilled to be able to recommend Ellen Dean's second book, *Communication Connection*. It is written to enrich communication in relationships, especially in marriages and families, but provides wisdom in all relational contexts.

I do not know of any other book on communication that covers all the meaningful aspects that are in this book. Neither do I know of another one that is as biblical, written from a counselor's perspective and experience, and is as practical and relevant as this book.

One of the unique and exciting characteristics of this book is a chapter called "Remember the Basics." Here Ellen reminds her readers of the lost art of listening. "Everyone wants to be, and deserves to be listened to, heard, and understood," she writes in Chapter 4.

May the wisdom and insight found in Ellen's latest book enable all of us to know more deeply the heart of the Father and His desire for us to authentically connect!

Steve Hardin, Lead Campus Pastor
White Rock Campus of LakePointe Church

I am honored to recommend Ellen Dean's new book, *Communication Connection,* to you. The author begins with her conviction that "the happiest marriages have great communication that improves and deepens through the years." She then weaves her career as a counselor and her personal faith walk into a guide to help couples get to that point. If you need communication help or are trying to help others who do, you will find this book a practical and powerful tool.

Ernie McCoulskey, Director of Missions
Kauf-Van Baptist Association

Ellen Dean has such a way with words. *Communication Connection* is a wealth of wisdom and insight that will add value to relationships just starting out, those that are seasoned, or those that are somewhere in between. What she has to say about the importance of communication within relationships brings clarity and order into muddled and chaotic seasons of life. Buy it! Read it! Live it! Words matter and Ellen Dean's will make a difference in how you choose and communicate yours.

Dr. David Rogers, Lead Pastor
Arapaho Road Baptist Church, Garland, Texas

I am grateful for Ellen Dean's biblical counseling ministry. *Communication Connection* is a practical resource organized around commonly encountered communication struggles. The case studies, wise counsel, and biblical truths in each chapter encouraged me personally in strengthening my marriage and will serve as a helpful resource for my pastoral family ministry.

Chad Selph, Senior Pastor
First Baptist Church, Allen, Texas

Communication Connection is an excellent tool for any couple looking to strengthen the "ties that bind" them together as a couple. I personally found the chapter on "Words that Build Up" convicting and encouraging. My wife and I get away annually to spend time together and to work on our marriage. We always read a book together about marriage to help get the conversation started. *Communication Connection* is the book we plan to read together this year—it is that good. It is my privilege to serve as Ellen Dean's pastor. I have seen Ellen and her husband, Bob, live out the principles taught in this book. She truly practices what she preaches, which adds authenticity to her words. I highly recommend this book for anyone who wants a better marriage—the kind of marriage that builds each other up and makes each other better.

Dr. Gary Singleton, Senior Pastor
The Heights Baptist Church, Richardson, Texas

Ellen Dean's book *Communication Connection* is a powerful and excellent resource to enrich communication in marriages and families. Ellen's counseling experience, passion to help relationships, and knowledge of what is necessary for positive and healthy communication all come together in this book. Her practical examples engage readers in interesting and compelling ways.

Ellen discusses biblical and practical characteristics of

communication, communicating with inspiration, building others up, and understanding and avoiding destructive communication patterns. She explains dynamics of conflicts and how to connect in meaningful ways for solutions and growth in marriage.

Ellen also shares how God has communicated in amazing ways declaring His love for us. I highly recommend *Communication Connection* for every marriage and family.

Pastor Steve Stroope
Lake Pointe Church, Rockwall, Texas

Communication does not come easy for most of us—especially within marriage relationships. In this book, Ellen shares timeless, practical biblical concepts and tools for improving communication within any relationship. Ministers, couples, or anyone seeking to improve their communication effectiveness can benefit from this wonderful resource.

Katie Swafford, M.A., L.P.C.-S., Ph.D. in Leadership
Director of Counseling Services with Texas Baptists

Ellen Dean, author of *Marriage Trust Builders*, has done it once again! It doesn't take a rocket scientist to know that marriage is all about communication, but how to do that is more difficult. Ellen's new book, *Communication Connection*, leads us through the process in a biblical, practical way. For that very reason I have sent folks to Ellen for counseling for years and will continue to do so. Thanks, Ellen, for another wonderful contribution in this all-important area.

Steve Swofford, Pastor
First Baptist Church, Rockwall, Texas

Ellen Dean has done it again! She has brought together a beautiful convergence of years of knowledge through her counseling experience, biblical guidance, and practical wisdom to help us all have better relationships. Never has there been a greater need in our uber polarized culture than now for us all to learn how to communicate better. Ellen knows that this starts in our personal relationships with one another, and she guides us to listen well, seek understanding, and love one another. This book will help you grow in the most important relationships in your life!

Dr. Jeff Warren, Senior Pastor
Park Cities Baptist Church, Dallas, Texas

DEDICATION

This book is dedicated to my precious husband, Bob, and to our wonderful grown children, Brian and Stephanie. They are all the best communicators I know. They always inspire and encourage me in every way.

Table of Contents

INTRODUCTION	xv
1. "WELL SAID"	1
2. AVENUES OF COMMUNICATION	13
3. SAY IT WITH INSPIRATION	27
4. REMEMBER THE BASICS	40
5. WORDS THAT BUILD UP	54
6. CONNECTING IN CONFLICTS	66
7. DESTRUCTIVE COMMUNICATION	81
8. USEFUL TOOLS, TECHNIQUES, AND REMINDERS	100
9. FREQUENTLY ASKED QUESTIONS ABOUT COMMUNICATION	114
10. THE MOST AMAZING COMMUNICATION	122

Introduction

EVERYONE CARES ABOUT communication. Meaningful communication connects people together and is vital to relationships. Communication is especially important in marriages and families. Communication is the magnetic quality that attracts people to each other and the glue that holds hearts together.

Communication is one of the best gauges of how spouses and family members feel cared for and valued. Confidence in how to talk together, express thoughts and emotions, and how to understand each other is foundational to growing loving marriages and relationships. The good news is that everyone can improve as a communicator.

Positive communication builds trust and well-being. Affirming communication in marriages and families is an important foundation for deepening relationships and providing joy. Constructive communication enables expressing ideas and feelings with the assurance of mutual esteem. It enables conflicts to be resolved in ways that strengthen and renew relationships.

Communication Connection was written to enrich marriages and families. Learning how to communicate appropriately and growing in communication skills gives relationships the commitment of love and grace. It enables individuals and couples to establish a connection that lasts a lifetime.

Communication Connection includes practical principles, helpful insights, and applicable tools to improve and strengthen the communication in marriages and families. It is filled with engaging case studies and examples that draw the attention of the readers, connecting them to practical life applications. Readers can identify with the examples and understand how to apply the principles.

All of the case studies that are included in this book are fictional narratives. None of them are real or of real people. Each example is a composite of many similar scenarios that people can connect with. They show how the principles apply to life, marriage and relationships. They are generic and yet engaging.

Communication Connection includes the importance of how positive communication helps gain a hearing and declares love and acceptance. Understanding how to say things in the best way makes relationships appealing. Methods and avenues of communication provide a broad scope of creative ways to share information and emotions.

Remembering the basics of listening, rhythm, and flow of conversations invites others for meaningful exchanges. Using words that build up, affirm, and express appreciation energizes healthy interactions. Communicating through serving, kindness, and compassion provides joy in relationships. Resolving conflicts respectfully builds trust, hope, and healing in relationships.

Committing to avoid destructive communication provides an atmosphere of emotional safety. Hurtful communication results in devastating effects for a long time and should be eliminated. Knowing useful tools and techniques helps people avoid snags and enables positive movement and understanding.

A magnificent display of God's communication is the heavens declaring the glory of the Lord. God's beautiful creation shows His power, order, and creativity.

The most amazing communication was when God sent His son, Jesus Christ, to Earth, proclaiming His love for us. Jesus Christ alone offers forgiveness for sins, abundant life now, and eternal life forever to all who choose to accept Him as their personal Savior.

Robert Keene and Mary Draper

Wedding Day—September 4, 1901

1

"WELL SAID"

"The words of a man's mouth are deep waters,
but the fountain of wisdom is a bubbling brook."
—Proverbs 18:4

HEART CONNECTION

IN THE LATE 1890s, Robert Keene and Mary Draper developed a heart connection through letters. He lived in Mississippi. She had moved from Mississippi to Texas. Mary had been friends with Robert's younger sisters. As an older teenager, Robert became responsible for his younger siblings after both of his parents died.

One summer Mary traveled back to Mississippi to visit her two friends Attie and Mattie Keene. Their older brother, Robert, noticed Mary and a close friendship developed. When summer ended, Mary went back to Texas to finish college and her relationship with Robert continued through correspondence.

After a year, some misunderstandings began to develop. The final straw came when Robert read in a letter that Mary had written to his sister and found out that she had met a "fellow." His next letter included news that he had found a girl named Mildred. They did not write again for eight months.

On the same day, January 25, 1897, both Robert and Mary wrote a letter to each other expressing their continuing interest while assuming the other person had probably found someone else. She apologized and told him that she did not have another fellow. Mary had written that she had received "attention from some Texas boys, but no one has touched my heart."

She asked Robert if he had married Mildred, and then signed her letter, "Your little Texas Sweetheart (I used to be)." He immediately wrote, "Dear Little Sweetheart, It does seem to be quite a coincidence that we both decided to 'make up' at the same time."

Concerning Mildred, he said, "I was only joking about Miss Mildred being my girl. She is Thurman's girl. He's been going to see her for more than a year." Robert admitted his "errors" and expressed his love to Mary. The letters continued until they married on September 4, 1901.

Robert made a hand-carved wooden box to keep over one hundred of their love letters, a box which still stores them today. Robert and Mary Keene were the great-grandparents of my husband, Bob. This sweet love story shows how vital communication is in relationships, sharing important information and bringing closeness.

COMMUNICATION IS VITAL TO RELATIONSHIPS

> A word aptly spoken is like apples of gold in settings of silver.
>
> (Proverbs 25:11)

Communication connects. God created us to be communicators. Even when communication may be physically or mentally limited, we still see efforts to connect in meaningful ways by whatever conduits of communication are available. Often amazing creativity is displayed when the yearning to communicate and connect exists.

Communication is conveying information, ideas, thoughts, and feelings. Communication is vital to all relationships. Different types of communication include verbal, nonverbal, body language, arts, actions, and written communications.

No one begins as a good communicator. Children adopt positive and negative communication from their family of origin. What if a person did not have a good example when growing up? No problem. Everyone can become a good communicator.

Thankfully, unhealthy negative patterns can be transformed with maturity when a person commits to positive growth. Caring more about others and desiring to be respectful helps communication improve. People learn to communicate based on observation, practicing good skills, and making positive communication a priority.

Impacts of communication cannot be overstated. Communication determines if people feel respected and loved or hurt and rejected. Everyone should want their communication to be positive and a blessing to others. That requires a selfless focus.

Relationships are part of God's marvelous plan for people. They are gifts from the Lord and are meant to produce joy, growth, meaning, strength, and blessings. Communication is the powerful component that draws people together.

Relationships are often described as positive or negative based on the quality of communication. Positive relationships can still have elements of negative communication at times. And negative relationships can be positive at times. However, generally, the greatest proportion will determine the description.

God created and designed marriage. His plan is that it be a growing relationship of special oneness. Caring, connecting communication results in a rich and joyful union. The happiest marriages have great communication that improves and deepens through the years.

When people love each other, they look forward to being together. They spend time doing things, continuously making plans to be together more. No one has to tell them to make their love a priority or to look forward to seeing each other. It's fun, enjoyable, important, and deliberate.

This is not just for young lovers or new relationships. Instead this also applies to seasoned marriages. The interest and delight should not diminish. Love should be unquenchable and regularly nurtured. Be committed to keeping communication alive and fresh by sharing and talking every day.

Cynthia and Clarence

Cynthia and Clarence talk past each other. They have frequent miscommunications and misunderstandings. Clarence shares limited details and is not diligent to discuss important information with Cynthia. She misses out on information about his job, family, and schedule. Clarence needs to accept responsibility for all the information he should be sharing with Cynthia.

Cynthia is often doing other things when Clarence is talking with her and gets distracted easily. She forgets some things he does tell her and is not good to follow up to make sure she fully hears everything. They both need to grow in communication skills.

BENEFITS OF IMPROVING COMMUNICATION

> He who guards his mouth and his tongue keeps himself from calamity.
> (Proverbs 21:23)

Communication draws people together and is foundational to meaningful relationships. As relationships blossom, the communication needs to be vibrant also. When communication is good, the relationship feels good. When it is uncomfortable or strained, the relationship feels painful or shallow.

Good communication requires commitment and emotional energy. Being willing to communicate says, "You are important to me." Couples need to be committed to discuss their thoughts and feelings. Making positive alterations brings powerful momentum and motivation toward renewal.

As a couple is open to communication growth, the marriage feels encouraged. Addressing what is said and how things are expressed, as well as the heart attitudes, is essential. Both spouses also need a willingness to discuss areas of selfishness that require confession and repentance.

Both spouses need to lay aside hurtful patterns and commit to kind communication. Everyone can benefit from learning new ways to express ideas and perspectives. Addressing the content and the methods of sharing offers positive improvement and growth.

Deliberately recalibrating to loving speech does not come naturally. Selflessness requires shifting your heart from personal desires to choosing to love others more. Hearts must be surrendered and focused on the Lord. Then it is easier to recognize thoughts and attitudes that need to be corrected.

A desire for improved communication and the commitment to speak positively even when it is difficult to do so proclaim, "I want to have a good relationship with you." This helps the recipient feel valued. Your spouse is worth it. The relationship is worth it.

When couples go to counseling, the most common presenting issue is to improve the communication in their relationship. Helping a couple learn to speak respectfully and listen with understanding will bring some immediate relief.

Though there are usually other issues to address as well, communication feels most critical. Improved communication improves relationships. When there is some kind of positive growth, it emotionally energizes one for more willingness to work on other areas.

Alex and Mary

Alex and Mary came into their marriage from a short dating time, without realizing the importance of deeper aspects of good communication. They did not initially think much of the conflict bouts they experienced early on. However, now they are feeling battle-worn and with limited confidence that things will improve.

Committing to counseling at least for a short term has helped them to diffuse the tension, hear each other better, and express thoughts and feelings. Their hearts are encouraged and willing to learn new skills. They realize the benefits of improving the communication.

GOOD COMMUNICATION BRINGS CLOSENESS IN RELATIONSHIPS

> Set a guard over my mouth, O Lord; keep watch
> over the door of my lips.
>
> (Psalm 141:3)

Communication is the component of the relationship that determines emotional closeness or distance. Often people describe the relationship in terms of how the communication is either meaningful and attentive or feels lonely and hurting.

Communicating clearly in a relationship can result in emotional openness. If there is a struggle to express thoughts and feelings, it can result in areas of guardedness. Comfortable communication is linked with feeling emotionally safe and being willing to be transparent.

Communication is important for all ages and relationships. Positive discussions result in meaningful emotions and a sense of acceptance. When dialogue is abrupt, unkind, or negative, the reaction and even the sense of self is affected.

If a neighbor impatiently addresses a child, or if an adult is spoken to rudely when ordering goods or services, either way, it is unsettling and results in people feeling devalued. This is even when the relationship is minimal. The impacts are greater when the relationship has significance.

People who care about others determine to communicate in the most respectful ways in every circumstance. None of us enjoys hearing unkind words. Rude messages push people away, and abrupt discussions shut people down. Bad communication does not reflect the innate value that everyone has.

One would think that understanding these principles results in positive communication all the time. But then life and humanity collide. People are often self-focused and express opinions negatively. Without caution, this leads to saying things that hurt feelings, sabotage relationships, and divert goodwill.

COMMUNICATION SHARES CONTENT IN RELATIONSHIPS

> Listen, for I have trustworthy things to say; I open my lips to speak what is right.
>
> (Proverbs 8:6)

Marriages need enough interesting content to maintain appropriate closeness. Information of many kinds is essential to give nourishment to help the relationship thrive. Regular, interesting discussions keep marriages informed, current, connected, and growing.

Marriages are filled with enriching areas and life together. There is a great wealth of topics to discuss and share, including family, friends, activities, work, goals, perspectives, feelings, thoughts, and opinions about everything. Spouses choosing to maintain flourishing conversations have vibrant marriages.

Those in close and healthy marriages feel like there are always so many things to share and discuss to enjoy rich conversations. Common interests keep spouses' hearts united, effervescent, and alive. The couple is committed to putting forth the energy and investment of developing interests and awareness in each other.

Yet some couples struggle to think of things to discuss. They report that they "have nothing to talk about." Marriage partners can lose touch if there is not enough effort made to remain curious about one another and invest in conversations about all areas of life.

Spouses need to continually build their repertoire of common interests in life. Branch out to explore new activities, hobbies, areas of service and skills. Limited desire to pursue the relationship is a problem that can debilitate a marriage.

Danette and Michael

Danette and Michael came into the relationship with individual hobbies already established. They agreed to continue with these and maintain a high level of individuality. Danette would spend time with crafts and sewing interests. Michael pursued hunting and outdoor hobbies.

Over time Michael and Danette have grown apart with little interest in what the other is doing and little unity in their marriage. It is not a surprise that they feel isolated in their relationship. It is important for Michael and Danette to develop some common interests and shared hobbies and activities to reignite their closeness.

PROBLEMS WHEN COMMUNICATION FALTERS

> All the words of my mouth are just; none of them is crooked or perverse.
>
> (Proverbs 8:8)

Lack of meaningful information shared by the relationship participants causes a loss of liveliness and progression in the relationship. Empty emotions and apathy take root when relationships are not encouraged, challenged, and enjoyed through compelling conversation.

When communication becomes strained or awkward, misunderstandings and miscommunications occur. Miscommunications result from confusing, incorrect messages and from inadequate content. Consequently, the listener has to rely on personal ability to connect the dots.

Relying on erroneous messages to make sense of the mixed-up batches of information rarely goes well and usually results in frustration on both sides. Resorting to assumptions robs the marriage of articulate conversation and enriching growth.

Misunderstandings happen when it is difficult to understand the "full picture." When this occurs, pause and ask questions, gaining information to understand the messages. Imagining or speculating about what was probably intended can mislead and bring complicating confusion.

Shared communication with desire, fervor, transparency, interesting material, and positive feedback is exciting and delightful. This also continuously invites the participants to share actively and enjoy content from the other participant.

Susan and Daniel

Susan and Daniel have been married for three years and have an infant eight months old. Daniel grew up in a quiet, reserved family and he struggles to express his thoughts and feelings. Susan grew up in a talkative family and usually overly expresses her feelings. In their marriage, Susan carried the major load in communication and felt emotionally weary.

Since the birth of their child, Daniel has stepped up in conversation and responsibilities. They are talking more as they parent together. They have committed to listen to each other, talk frequently, and pursue each other consistently. Daniel is expressing more, and Susan is listening more. Both are feeling more deeply in love.

POWERFUL IMPACTS OF POSITIVE COMMUNICATION

> The lips of the righteous nourish many, but fools
> die for lack of judgment.
>
> (Proverbs 10:21)

Good communication is foundational to a healthy marriage. It can become sweeter if the participants are willing to grow, make changes, and seek to honor the other person lovingly. Commitment to the quality and quantity of meaningful communication is priceless.

Significant communication deepens the relationship. It results from spending quality time and effort in verbal discussions. It is important for the marriage partners to be willing to work at improving conversing, sharing in the relationship, and expressing thoughts, ideas, and opinions clearly.

Cameron and Shonda

Cameron and Shonda came into their marriage with a strong commitment to focus on growing in their communication and to spend time talking daily. They agreed to resolve conflicts as they arise, give each other the benefit of the doubt, and share about everything.

Their marriage has not been perfect, and they have had times of recommitting to these values and learning new conversational skills. But now, years into the marriage, there is a joy that they have continued to make it a priority and to act in love with each other. Their positive communication has given immense value to the relationship.

2

AVENUES OF COMMUNICATION

A man of knowledge uses words with restraint,
and a man of understanding is even-tempered.

- Proverbs 17:27

SAY IT WITH YOUR EYES

EYES ARE COMPELLING physical aspects of people. Eye contact is important to communication and attentiveness. Looking at a person's eyes is respectful and affirms, "You matter to me. I am focusing on you." Every person wants and deserves focused attention.

We often say, "Look each other in the eye," or "Let me see your eyes" when we want assurance of someone's attention.

Eyes show sincere interest and emotional alignment. Looking directly at someone is powerful for emotional connection.

Our culture is full of looking away, keeping our eyes down, and not looking directly at people. This leads to increased aloneness and isolation. Choosing to make kind eye contact is meaningful in feeling noticed.

Kindly giving eye contact when talking with your spouse or family member is loving and considerate. Willfully withholding it feels to the other like rejection and disregard. This can hinder some emotional trust in the relationship.

Many people think they can at least partially determine another person's truthfulness by how they look directly at them when talking. "I can tell in your eyes if you're being honest or not." This is a common statement when someone is looking for trustworthiness.

> The eye is the lamp of the body. If your eyes are good,
> your whole body will be full of light.
>
> (Matthew 6:22)

Derrick and Mona

Derrick feels like Mona does not value him or the marriage. When they are having conversations, Mona often takes out her phone and gets distracted.

Even recently when they went out to eat at a nice restaurant for their anniversary, Mona started looking at her phone and responding to non-urgent texts from her friends.

Derrick feels deflated and discouraged. Monica does not give meaningful eye contact when she and Derrick are talking together. He feels like this reflects her feelings about him and their marriage.

SAY IT WITH YOUR TOUCH AND BODY LANGUAGE

Communication is more than just words and discussion. Your physical touch is a powerful way of expressing loving kindness with people you care about. Sometimes when there are not words to say what needs to be said, an appropriate touch can communicate volumes.

There was a time when Jesus reached out and touched a man with leprosy. His touch showed His love for the man. Leprosy was a horrible disease, and no one was to touch a leprous person. Those with leprosy had to live alone and isolated outside of town.

However, when Jesus met this man, He reached out and touched him. Probably the man had not felt a human touch in years. Yet, Jesus wanted to communicate to the man that he was loved (Luke 5:12-13). Jesus communicates that same love to us today.

Appropriate physical touch can communicate love, comfort, and kindness. Your touch can be assuring and encouraging. Let your words and your touches be congruent, kind, and thoughtful. Physical touch adds dimension to communication.

Affection is physical touch in marriage that gently reaches out and speaks volumes of love without saying a word. Affection should not be just a step leading to sexual intimacy. Rather, it is the tender moments of hand holding, endearing hugs, sweet kisses, and being physically close. Every day should have lots of affection separate from sexual intimacy.

Most wives value affection even more than sexual intimacy. Husbands may hope for sexual intimacy more often. Husbands need to realize that expectations for sexual activity in marriage without large daily quantities of nonsexual affection makes the relationship feel emotionally lacking to the wife.

Affection says, "I love you," in many ways. It is not overrated. It draws a couple closer and is a strong sustaining element in the marriage. Develop consistent caring affection in your marriage to communicate the deep love you feel for your spouse. It will help the love grow even more.

Harsh and angry physical expressions tear down communication and hurt relationships. Physical touch that is impatient, frustrated, or selfish causes severe harm and must be avoided. If you are that angry person, you must change and never do that again. Get help from a biblical counselor or minister.

If you are married to a person who exhibits anger physically, tell others. Your safety is crucial. Go to others for help. Inappropriate physical touch is not okay and needs to be stopped. Seek help from law enforcement, a minister, or a counselor.

Body language adds to what is being communicated. However, do not try to interpret it too precisely. Some people rely excessively on evaluating body language and get mixed messages. If you have uncertainties, ask questions to clarify. There may be inconsistencies in what is spoken and what the body portrays.

The discrepancies between verbal communications and body language are called incongruent messages. When there is a contradiction, the body language is believed the most. Match your messages to build trust in your communication. Body language should not contradict your words.

Lance and Leslie

Lance pulls Leslie close affectionately when he wants sex. At other times, when Leslie just wants to be affectionate, Lance pushes her away and says he doesn't like so much touching. Leslie feels hurt and thinks Lance's physical affection is not about how he loves her, but rather to attract for sexual intimacy. She feels unloved and disrespected.

SAY IT WITH YOUR EMOTIONS— EXPRESS YOUR LOVE

> A new command I give you: Love one another.
> As I have loved you, so you must love one another.
> (John 13:34)

Emotions are a gift from God. The assortment and conglomeration of emotions are extraordinary characteristics of who we are as people. Emotions help us feel and experience life, events, and relationships. Emotions are a rich part of who we are individually and how we relate to others.

Our emotions help connect us with God and with people. How we experience all the ups and downs and ins and outs of life show a lot about us. Emotions clarify perceptions and are attached to how one views what happens and how it impacts each person. However, emotions are limiting and not reliable.

God did not give us emotions to guide life or to be our major decision makers. It can be concerning to trust emotions when we are trying to live life in a wise and prudent way. Emotions can be beguiling and misleading.

Our mental abilities are separate from our emotions. God

gave us our mind and our will to help us make decisions in life. It is with our cognitive skills that we can make right and positive choices. It is with our mind that we have discernment and wisdom.

Using mental abilities exclusively results in limited emotional input and seems flat or "matter of fact." Utilizing mostly the emotional aspect may seem questionable and lacking wise stability. Relationships flourish with balanced and healthy emotional and mental contributions.

Learning to appropriately experience and express emotions can bring a bountiful harvest for strong and loving relationships. Learn how to put thoughts and feelings into words so that others can know you better, more fully. Take time to know others as well. Begin first to enrich your marriage.

There is an old adage where a non-expressive spouse says, "I told you I loved you when I married you, and if I change my mind, I'll let you know." That it is not very humorous or relational. It is a sad example of people who are not willing to invest in marriage to keep it vibrant.

Relational laziness results in hurting marriages and broken hearts. There is no excuse for this kind of neglect and disdain. Individuals who value their low-key approach don't want to have to put important effort into the relationship.

These individuals are not caring toward other's needs and desires. They are self-focused and think status quo is enough and sustainable. They are mistaken. They will reap loneliness in others, callousness in themselves, and will miss the immense blessings that God designed for marriage and families.

Loving is caring for the other person more than self and acting in the other's best interest. For example, it would be wrong if someone said, "I don't express love much because I don't really need it." No one should treat others according to one's own preferences.

That is irrelevant and unkind. A person's level of communication should not be based on your own needs and desires. It should be based on what is special and meaningful for that person who is the object of your love and interactions, not yourself.

Marriages, above all others, and then families need to be nourished and nurtured. They need to have love expressed with great energy and in many multiple creative ways regularly and consistently. Be proactive, diligent, believable, and authentic. Be known as the one who expresses love freely and generously.

Love with a willingness to be "poured out" for those whom God has given to you. Love selflessly, joyfully, energetically, devotedly, and unceasingly. The importance of this cannot be overstated. God commands this, others certainly deserve this, and you will find joy in it.

We should live our lives to have the least regrets. You will have less remorse if at the end of your life you have loved well and deeply. If you care about others at all, you can have great sorrow later if your love was stingy and minimal.

Your feelings matter. Other people's feelings matter. Learning how to understand the role of emotions to strengthen your marriage requires a great deal of wisdom and discernment. Seek God's Word for guidance in following His example.

Fred and Alaina

Fred and Alaina struggle to connect in communication. He enjoys talking about everything, but conversations soon fall limp. Alaina does not feel like she knows what to say. She feels like her contributions do not measure up to his interest level. Her focus on her own fear of sharing limits their relational closeness.

Fred has no expectations about how she should respond. He only wants to be discussing things together. His tender kindness patiently invites her back into conversations, and he listens to her perspective. She grows in confidence and excitement.

Alaina realizes that her concerns about her ability cause her to waste meaningful couple connection. When she chooses to put her attention on caring about Fred and not worrying about what she will say, communication becomes easier.

SAY IT WITH YOUR MOUTH — IT'S YOUR TURN TO TALK

The definition of a good communicator is a person who expresses himself or herself with right words and in right ways. It is a special communicator who can share about significant things. It is a kind person who can invite others into the conversation to contribute as well.

Moving toward the relationship to capitalize on times to talk says, "I will talk about what you want to talk about because you matter to me." Don't let other reasons delay you from pursuing important conversations with those you love.

Don't expect your spouse to always reach out for you. Sharing the initiative is meaningful to both spouses. Put forth the energy to engage in regular meaningful communication. Let your actions say, "I love you enough to pursue you in conversation." Avoiding communication is not kind or loving.

All relationship participants should assume responsibility for communication. No one should have to plead with the other to talk or open up. A regular unwillingness or procrastination to discuss and share can cause the other spouse to feel weary and choose to emotionally disconnect.

Each spouse needs to place a high priority on the marital partner. A willingness to engage, converse, dialogue, and show interest is vital to the relationship. Paying attention, listening to your spouse, and involving yourself in meaningful conversations strengthen the marriage and deepen the emotional intimacy.

When a marriage partner seems uncaring, is often preoccupied with something or someone else, and delays or avoids conversations, the spouse feels marginalized. This can possibly result in detachment and hurt feelings. It is disappointing and sad when the communication feels one-sided with a lack of mutual investment.

If you are the spouse or family member who struggles to communicate, the good news is that people can become better communicators. It takes diligence and a commitment to engage emotionally. It requires focusing on loving the other person instead of your own personal hesitancies.

It is common to hear, "I just can't say what I want to say," "I have trouble putting my thoughts and feelings into words," or "I have difficulty talking like I wish I could." These are understandable and valid. However, the thoughts need to be corrected or they can rob the relationship of positive dialogue.

A person's heart is obvious in how he or she converses with others, or not. For example, "It's not worth the effort." "What will people think of me?" "How will I look?" These are examples of self-focus. Genuinely shift your attention to the other person. Act in love and this will help you to forget yourself.

The healthiest and most satisfying communication is when

there is strong effort from the participants for voluntary and diligent investment in the relationship. To the degree that the participants feel that each person is pursuing the relationship with respect and commitment, the effort results in feelings of closeness, value, and safety.

Melissa and Frank

Melissa feels angry, and Frank feels despondent in their marriage. She feels like he is selfish and uncaring. He feels like she comes down too hard on him.

Early on in the marriage, he was slow in communicating and did not recognize the necessity of meaningful discussion. She would talk, trying to encourage conversation. As he deferred to her more and communicated less, she grew angry.

They are at a stalemate. Frank needs to confess and apologize for his lack of effort since early in their marriage. He needs to actively and energetically communicate with Melissa without giving up. She needs to patiently slow down her talking and listen as he communicates.

SAY IT WITH RELATIONSHIP MOTIVATION

> Instead, speaking the truth in love, we will in all things
> grow up into him who is the Head, that is, Christ.
> (Ephesians 4:15)

Each person should be devoted to communicating in loving ways. Spouses and family members invest in the relationship when they feel positive connections. Relationships still periodically experience difficulty and struggles, but there is a sense of positive rapport.

Marriages need comprehensive daily talk times. Communicating fully about issues as they arise maintains marital closeness. Resist the natural inclination to let the busyness of our world limit communication to only schedules and daily activities.

Early in our marriage my husband gave me a gift with the commitment that every day we would talk for as long as we wanted or needed and about anything we desired. This commitment has been honored consistently through these past forty-six years. The benefits have been immeasurable. It has proven to be one of the most beautiful aspects of our marriage. We both treasure these times.

Couples need deep conversation to stay current, solve conflicts promptly, share feelings and perspectives, and continue to grow as a couple. Wives hunger for meaningful conversation with their husbands. This is a major component of trust and emotional closeness to them.

Couples need to intentionally put thoughts and feelings into words so the other spouse can know. Share information, then in deeper levels to pursue understanding. Commit personally to being willing to share deeply, and invite your spouse to do the same.

In my counseling, I frequently hear from a spouse that the other spouse just doesn't talk. This produces feelings of disconnection and sad loneliness in the marriage. Communicating freely and willingly says, "You are special to me." Giving the effort, energy, and emotion toward the relationship keeps it connected and valuable.

When partners in a marriage become lackadaisical about

investing in the relationship, they find the relationship quickly becomes cold and out of touch. What should be woven together is now detached and separated. There should be quick remedial actions to find times to talk, share openly, and listen intently to catch up.

Humble yourself to acknowledge your part in the lack of communication and closeness. This can help to reestablish the unity, connection, and commitment. Do not waste time being lazy or selfish. If your spouse is the one pulling away, seek outside godly help.

Randall and Suzanne

Randall felt like his conversations with Suzanne were one-sided, with him doing all the work. Regardless of what the topic or circumstance was, Suzanne would participate only minimally. Randall would ask her questions. She would shrug but remain quiet.

Randall began to explain to Suzanne that her willingness to communicate is an indication of her commitment to the relationship. She chose to change and invest emotionally and commit to proactive communication. Their marriage is growing in depth and vitality.

SAY IT IN WRITING

There are many ways that a spouse or a family member can put thoughts and feelings into written words to convey meaningfully to those they love. In today's world, devices have greatly replaced other ways of communicating.

The more traditional ways of poetry, music, cards, love

letters, and sweet notes still have great value in relationships. You may think you are not very creative, but creativity is not the most important aspect in the romance expressions. Rather, it is love for the other person and the desire to declare that love. Go ahead, give it a whirl. Write a poem or a song to express some significant things to people you care about.

Surprise them! It will be a joy and a blessing to them. It will be fun for you and will give you a memorable sense of accomplishment. You may find that you are more creative than you anticipated. Encourage someone with your written words. Leave a legacy of love.

The Song of Songs in the Bible is an ancient love story. Listen to the descriptions of the Beloved and the Lover and their love for each other.

> Beloved
> "Listen! My Lover!
> Here he comes,
> leaping across the mountains,
> bounding over the hills.
> My beloved is like a gazelle or a young stag.
> Look! There he stands behind our wall,
> gazing through the windows,
> peering through the lattice.
> My beloved spoke and said to me,
> 'Arise, my darling,
> my beautiful one, come with me.'"
> (Song of Solomon 2:8-10)
> Lover
> "How beautiful you are, my darling!
> Oh, how beautiful!

Your eyes behind your veil are doves.
Your hair is like a flock of goats
descending from the hills of Gilead.
Your teeth are like a flock of sheep just shorn,
coming up from the washing.
Each has its twin;
not one of them is alone.
Your lips are like a scarlet ribbon;
your mouth is lovely."
(Song of Solomon 4:1-3)

3

SAY IT WITH INSPIRATION

Pleasant words are a honeycomb,
sweet to the soul and healing to the bones.
—Proverbs 16:24

SAY IT WITH ENCOURAGEMENT

HOW WE COMMUNICATE is more than simply the words and expressions we use. Communication encompasses other aspects on a deeper lever. The most extraordinary communicators are also known for how positive they are in their daily attitudes and outlooks.

Their reputations are described by how they seek God, value life, have wisdom, exhibit kindness, and care for other people. They are labeled as "encouragers," "life-givers," and "joy-bringers." People agree that to have that reputation description would represent living life on a significant level.

People remember and appreciate encouragers in their lives. Everyone has struggles in life. To navigate these times alone is formidable. When someone steps up to walk alongside, share wise advice, help carry our burden, or speak words of encouragement, life seems brighter. The darkness dissipates, the storm lightens, and our hearts are filled with hope.

If you were invited to become an encourager to someone else, would that feel like a worthy and valuable aspiration? Indeed, it would be. The Bible teaches us to love and encourage one another (Hebrews 10:23). This verse teaches us to encourage one another toward good works.

When we have a personal relationship with Jesus Christ and belong to Him, He lives through us. We can experience His presence and comfort in our own life and share that with others. God uses that to be uplifting to others.

An encourager honors God and blesses others. Your heart will smile with joy when your words of hope and faith inspire others. Proclaiming encouragement is one of the highest and noblest forms of communication. Choose to be a person who follows God, shares His love, and shows the hope He gives. Be an encourager.

SAY IT WITH HONESTY

> The integrity of the upright guides them,
> but the unfaithful are destroyed by their duplicity.
> (Proverbs 11:3)

Honesty is an important characteristic for any person. Honest communication produces trustworthiness and believability. Individuals are known for whether they are reliable or not, based on whether they are truthful or not.

God requires honesty. He hates lying. Truthfulness is absolutely essential. God expects us to be completely honest in relationships. The most important relationships are marriage and family. Honesty and trustworthiness are exceptionally essential in those relationships.

> There are six things the LORD hates, seven that are detestable to him:
> haughty eyes, a lying tongue, hands that shed innocent blood,
> a heart that devises wicked schemes, feet that are quick to rush into evil,
> a false witness who pours out lies and a man who stirs up dissension among brothers.
> (Proverbs 6:16-19)

Trust is foundational to healthy marriages. Honesty is crucial in marriage. Dishonesty on any level breaks trust. Lies and deceit corrupt and cripple the marriage. The marriage becomes stagnant and stymied, shutting down healthy bonds and emotions. The marriage is in a high-risk crisis.

When a spouse lies, immediate steps need to be taken to rescue the marriage. A good resource to help couples with this struggle is *Marriage Trust Builders* by Ellen Dean. *Marriage Trust Builders* is a biblical and practical guide for strengthening and restoring the trust in marriage.

It is written for hurting couples and for the counselors, ministers, friends, and family members who care for hurting couples. Everyone knows someone who has a hurting marriage.

Perhaps it is your coworker, your neighbor, or your family member, or maybe it is you.

Marriage Trust Builders is an excellent resource to give and receive. Order it from any bookstore or go to www.ellendeanbooks.com. The last third of the book describes ways to invest in marriages. This is a great resource for marriages, and ministers and counselors who work with couples.

Honest communication in marriage involves truthful words and authentic messages throughout the relationship. These include congruent information, expressions, body language, and actions. Spouses need to have absolute confidence that their marriage partner is transparent, accountable, and fully trustworthy.

Samuel and Lana

Samuel and Lana spend a lot of time debating the facts. Samuel feels confused and exasperated. All through their marriage he has noted that Lana's narratives do not match the facts. Recently, the inconsistencies seem to be increasing.

Samuel confronts Lana, but she shirks him off, accuses him of being petty, says he is "not listening" to her, and that he is "not trusting" her.

Samuel asks Lana about the questionable financial records; discrepancies in her scheduling and reporting of events; questionable information he hears from family and friends; and about the unverifiable descriptions Lana tells him. She has no credible explanations.

SAY IT WITH YOUR FAITH

One of the most assuring ways of communicating in marriage and other relationships is the expression of faith in God. Life can blindside us with unexpected events. Even as I write, our country is in a state of emergency because of the COVID-19 virus.

Uncertainty and difficulties can be emotionally debilitating. When a trusted person kindly walks alongside those who are hurting, expressing empathy and support, hearts are lifted. God is bigger than every problem we face, and He cares about every detail of life.

Expressing faith to people in their times of confusion, fear, or grief invites them to look to God for the power and help that He alone can give. Understanding an individual's emotions and gently turning the attention to rely on God provide immense comfort.

Spouses and family members should care about the emotions of the other spouse and others. Trusting in God helps us to focus on the real source of assurance and courage. One of the most endearing characteristics of family members or friends is their ability to fortify our faith in God.

Encouraging faith is an important form of communication. Viewing life through the lens of trusting God and His plan shifts the attention from personal emotions and circumstances to a larger view of God's sovereignty and guidance. Choosing to trust God in painful circumstances requires faith.

Bernard and Carmen

Bernard and Carmen left town for the weekend to go

take care of Bernard's ill mother in a nearby city. They drove through a heavy rainstorm on the way there. Soon after they arrived, they received a phone call from some of their neighbors back home. Lightning struck their house and it burned to the ground.

In the following weeks, as they sorted through the ashes and tried to regroup, they were an inspiration to family and friends. They were steadfast in their faith and optimistic in their outlook. Clearly, God was giving them grace to walk through this devastating circumstance. They were trusting God to meet their needs.

Believing God means placing our confidence and faith in Him instead of ourselves and our abilities. Every time we commit to that, we experience God's peace. We are changed, and the peace of God guards our hearts and minds.

> And the peace of God, which transcends all understanding,
> will guard your hearts and your minds in Christ Jesus.
>
> (Philippians 4:7)

We receive comfort from God in all of our struggles. That is the same comfort that we can then share with others to help them in any difficulty they face. The events don't have to match. It is the comfort from God that applies to all circumstances.

> Praise be to the God and Father of our Lord Jesus Christ,
> the Father of compassion and the God of all comfort,

> who comforts us in all our troubles, so that we can comfort those
> in any trouble with the comfort we ourselves have received from God.
> For just as the sufferings of Christ flow over into our lives,
> so also through Christ our comfort overflows.
>
> (2 Corinthians 1:3-5)

Grow in your faith. When others are struggling and need a helping hand, you can show them a loving God and Savior. Jesus Christ meets people where they are when they turn to Him. He allows us to be encouraging blessings to others.

The following verse is repeated all through the Bible. In the New Testament, Jesus was asked, "What is the most important commandment?" Jesus answered that the most important one is the one below.

> Love the Lord your God with all your heart and with all your soul
> and with all your mind and with all your strength.
> The second is this: "Love your neighbor as yourself."
> There is no commandment greater than these.
>
> (Mark 12:30-31)

We are instructed to love God with all our heart, soul, mind, and strength. We are to love God first and most, over and above anyone and anything else. Motivation to love God produces obeying and honoring Him in our life. When we get this in focus, it transforms everything.

The result is that we love other people more than we love ourselves. Loving God rightly helps us to genuinely care more about other's best interests than our own. A compassionate and sacrificial love is a witness of our love for God. It shows others that we are surrendered to Jesus Christ and want to live for Him.

Hopefully, others will see extraordinary love in us and want to know Jesus Christ also. Be sure to tell them with words about Jesus Christ. Your actions alone are not enough. Proclaiming about Jesus Christ is the most significant and compassionate communication we can ever share because of the impact on a person's eternal life.

SAY IT WITH THANKFULNESS IN CIRCUMSTANCES

An attitude of thankfulness is one of the most powerful traits. It has a magnetic quality in relationships and invites people to draw near. Conversely, someone who is a grumbler and a complainer repels people.

Interestingly enough, both characteristics are willful choices that have a large impact on the individual's heart and relationship with others. This heart attitude is usually more evident to others than to self. Assess yourself. Recommit to the right choice of thankfulness.

Expressing gratitude for your spouse, family, and others says you care about them. This is one of the most impactful ways of communicating. Gratitude is one of the strongest relational connectors and motivates people to continue to do good.

Margot and Nathan

During this pandemic season, Margot and Nathan are home with their children. Margot is a teacher and provides instruction to her classroom online daily. She also homeschools their own children. Nathan was in sales and lost his job shortly after the shutdown began. He is now helping to homeschool their children as he looks for another job.

Nathan has kept a thankful attitude toward God and his family. He is grateful for all of their blessings. Nathan is modeling for his family and friends how to trust in God even in difficult circumstances. His thankful attitude helps Margot and their children to trust God and remember their many blessings.

> Be joyful always; pray continually; give thanks in all circumstances,
> for this is God's will for you in Christ Jesus.
> (1 Thessalonians 5:16-18)

Life is filled with curveballs. How we choose to respond in these times exposes a great deal about our heart. The good news is that a person can choose his or her attitude and outlook. As we choose to have a thankful heart and share this with others, we extend hope in tough times.

It is difficult to choose thankfulness and a positive attitude, but the results can be life changing. Committing to be a grateful person who sees good, enriches relationships, brings joy, encourages others, and shares hope produces a healthier life.

Seeing the potential to be a positive influence on others and to increase the quality of our own life is compelling. Choose joy in your heart, put it on your face for others to see, and share it with your words and actions. Communicating a thankful attitude is contagious.

SAY IT WITH CONFESSION AND FORGIVENESS

We are all sinners and we all make mistakes at times. How we respond to our spouse and family members during the times when they make mistakes really reveals our own personal walk with the Lord. Do we respond with grace and mercy, or are we harsh and accusing?

Sins are wrong. They should not be condoned or brushed off and need to be addressed and acknowledged. When we sin against each other, there should be honest confession with the commitment for repentance. Then restore the trust by following through on your commitment for change.

> Therefore, confess your sins to each other and pray for each other so that you may be healed. The prayer of a righteous man is powerful and effective.
>
> (James 5:16)

James 5:16 says to confess your sins to each other and pray for each other so that you may be healed. Confession and apologies are very important. Sincerely asking for forgiveness and granting it to each other brings healing to your hearts and relationship. This honors God and will bless you and your spouse.

If you are the one who has sinned against your spouse or family member, understand the hurt feelings and broken trust you have caused. Express your remorse genuinely; confess willingly and completely. Replace your sinful behaviors with what is right and good.

Words and actions need to honor God and be loving to others. Focus on your part and the changes you must make. Do not say to others they should forgive you. That is not your responsibility and should not be your concern. Let your repentance build new trust in the hearts of your spouse and family members.

Repentance means to stop sinning. Turn and go in the opposite direction. Change your wrong words and actions. Replace them with right attitudes and behaviors. Repent consistently in an ongoing way. Let your repentance build new trust in the hearts of your spouse and family toward you.

If you are the one who has been sinned against, allow your spouse to apologize and prove to you there will be significant change in heart and actions. As repentance is evident in your spouse's actions and words, affirm the good changes. Extend forgiveness to your spouse as Jesus Christ forgives us.

> Bear with each other and forgive whatever grievances
> you may have against one another. Forgive as the Lord forgave you.
> (Colossians 3:13)

God forgives us when we ask Him, and He instructs us to forgive. God, in offering salvation to us, has forgiven us for much more than we have to forgive others who sin against us. Give others a chance to prove that they will change actions and attitudes and will work to do whatever is necessary to rebuild the trust in the relationship.

> Be kind and compassionate to one another,
> forgiving each other, just as in Christ God forgave
> you.
>
> (Ephesians 4:32)

Jesus Christ died for the sins of everyone in the world. He forgives everyone who asks Him for forgiveness. God shows us amazing grace when we sin against him. God hates sin, but He loves all people. Jesus Christ died on the cross to pay the penalty for sin. No one could do this for us except Jesus Christ. However, it is important to confess our sins to God and ask Him for forgiveness.

> If we claim to be without sin, we deceive
> ourselves,
> and the truth is not in us. If we confess our sins,
> he is faithful and just
> and will forgive us our sins and purify us from all
> unrighteousness.
>
> (1 John 1:8-9)

When we confess our sins and ask God for forgiveness, He is faithful and just to forgive us our sins and to restore us to righteousness. The cross is big enough to cover all our sins. God wants us to believe that He fully forgives us just as He said He would do. We cannot see this forgiveness, but we receive it by faith, because God promised it.

God takes our sins away. The Bible has a beautiful metaphor of God removing our sins as far as the east is from the west. The east and west never meet. God gives us a fresh start. Then He helps us to live for Him and to know the joys of a close relationship with Him. This is one of the greatest blessings imaginable.

> As far as the east is from the west, so far has he removed our transgressions from us.
> (Psalm 103:12)

In marriages and in families, people hurt one another. Sometimes it is on purpose. Sometimes it is inadvertently. We feel conviction from the Holy Spirit when we have sinned. Perhaps also our spouse, a family member, or someone else tells us that we have sinned.

When you become aware of it, you need to confess and apologize. Make a commitment that you will not do it again. Ask those loved ones for forgiveness. Prove your commitment by living in a trustworthy and loving way with your spouse and family members.

When others sin against you and then confess and ask for forgiveness, how should you respond? Jesus Christ instructs us to forgive others who have sinned against us. Show grace because Jesus Christ shows grace to us. Even when your heart hurts, you can offer forgiveness.

Forgiveness does not mean your emotions do not still hurt. Neither does it mean that the wrong actions are not important or that you condone the sins. Rather it means you give the pain and injustice to God and trust Him to deal with it.

Forgiveness acknowledges God's forgiveness to us for salvation. Then we extend that grace to others. God also tells the sinner to repent and walk in loving righteousness with changed behavior.

4

REMEMBER THE BASICS

> Whatever you have learned or received or heard from me or seen in me—
> put it into practice. And the God of peace will be with you.
>
> —Philippians 4:9

IN MANY AREAS of life, we have to remember the basics in order to do a good job and have a positive experience. This is true of sports, recreational activities, work projects, and many other areas. We are required to remember the necessary tools and how to use them for the best and most effective results.

Similarly, in communication, implementing the basic skills provides for the most relational connection. It is easy to begin to lay aside these basic skills and applications unless there is a deliberate plan to retain them. This results in wounded feelings, confusion, muddled messages, conflicts, and broken hearts.

Some of the basics we want to remember with communication include listening, taking turns talking, putting thoughts and feelings into words, caring about the other person, addressing issues, and talking calmly and respectfully.

LISTENING

> He who answers before listening—that is his folly
> and his shame.
>
> (Proverbs 18:13)

The phrase "Can you hear me now?" has become a very common statement in our culture. With the permeation of cell phones, we are often trying to find a place where we can have a good connection for a phone call.

Listening in communication has two aspects. First it involves listening to how our communication sounds to others. Hopefully, we can be aware of miscommunications and problems, and remedy them in a timely way with constructive corrections.

Everyone wants and deserves to be listened to, heard, and understood. Knowing how to listen is a basic building block for good communication, but it does not come naturally. To be named a good listener is a high compliment to which everyone should aspire.

Listening means an attentiveness to what the other person is saying, waiting to speak until they finish, and then responding in a polite way. Listening requires pausing to allow the other person to complete some thoughts they want to express before you take over the talking.

Listening is a way of honoring a person. It says, "You and what you are sharing are important to me." Patient and attentive listening allows the other person to express what they desire to say. Focusing only on what you are about to say limits respectful listening.

If someone says you are not listening, stop right then, apologize, and focus on that person. Suggest that you can jot some words down while they are talking to remind you of what you want to say later instead of interrupting. Let the other person know that what they want to say is important to you.

Writing down a few key words helps you then quickly put your attention back on the speaker. It also helps you remember what you want to say later when it is your turn to talk. Both of you have essential things to say. Commit to listen completely to what the other person wants to say.

Listening involves the capacity to hear on a deeper level. Listen to your spouse's heart and to others you love. Try to listen for the expressed or non-expressed emotions. Listen to the tone, to the downcast or upbeat nuances, and to feelings of delight or exasperation.

Listen to connect with the person and what is being said. Give them the blessing of being valued. Let good listening be your strong suit and reputation. Remember, you have two ears and one mouth. Use proportionately.

Bernice and Duncan

Bernice and Duncan are both committing to grow in communication skills in their marriage. Historically, Bernice is not a good listener and does not give appropriate attention to what

Duncan says. Duncan feels slighted and minimized.

Duncan frequently interrupts Bernice and inserts what he wants to say without letting Bernice finish. He is thinking more of what he wants to add than what her thoughts and feelings are. Bernice feels cut off and devalued.

TAKE TURNS—AVOID INTERRUPTING

> Each of you should look not only to your own interests,
> but also to the interests of others.
>
> (Philippians 2:4)

"Please don't interrupt me." Do you ever hear that? This could be a warning sign that you are interrupting more than you realize and hopefully more than you want to. We are often unaware of the extent that we may be seen as an interrupter.

Do you like trying to talk with someone who interrupts? They do not let you finish your thought or sentence. It's aggravating to say the least. It feels like nothing is as important to them as what they are saying.

Check yourself. Ask others to monitor you. Believe the results they report. The pattern of frequently interrupting others can easily creep up on you. The best reminders to stop are your love for others and your desire to be respectful. Those are powerful and appropriate motivations.

METHOD AND AMOUNT ARE IMPORTANT

> Simply let your "Yes" be "Yes," and your "No,"
> "No";

anything beyond this comes from the evil one.

(Matthew 5:37)

When communicating, you can give the big picture so listeners can have an overall view for the discussion. "Start with the bottom line" is a request for a general description and then moving to the specifics.

Before conversations, one can jot down major bullet points to be discussed and show the list to the other person. Seeing designated points can actually help the other person feel a relief that this list is doable. Limit the times things are stated in the same conversation. Avoid over emphasizing "just to be clear."

In communication, be respectful so that you are not repeating things. Some communicators believe that what they have to say is important and worth repeating several times. Repetition causes the listeners to doubt that you think they understand. It feels boring and condescending.

Use alternative tools to assure that others are following what you are saying. Good eye contact and involving the listeners along the way give a sense of their tracking with you. Some tools can be reflective listening and summarizing. These are described in the "Tools and Techniques" chapter.

People listening to repeated communications say it feels like control and manipulation. Emotional and verbal abuse encompasses repeating information. This is seen in lecture form, and the listeners are required to stay and listen to what the speaker wants to say for as long as the lecturer wants to talk. It can continue for long periods of time, even hours.

Sometimes a speaker thinks it's good to talk and explain until the listener agrees. It is not healthy to feel the need to convince others fully before the conversation can wind down.

This is destructive and dysfunctional. If you are on the receiving end of this, you may want to seek outside help with a minister or a counselor.

"Bundling" is a common term regarding combining many services. However, it is not beneficial when it comes to communication. Be clear and concise. Avoid discussing several topics at one time. That is confusing and not productive.

The expression "Don't throw in the kitchen sink" is a request to stop talking about several issues all at once. Prioritize topics you want to discuss. "Piling on" can happen when a person talks fast, trying to say everything needed.

Perhaps that person feels he or she does not have many opportunities to share and hold their spouse's attention. Give genuine assurance to your spouse that you care about what he or she wants to say. Encourage slowing down the conversation and reassure your spouse that you will listen.

Zach and Tina

Tina has learned to minimize what she says and how she responds to Zach. It seems like no matter what the circumstance or topic of discussion, Zach likes to capture the center of attention and hold it for great lengths of time until he is finished talking. Zach likes to go on and on.

When Zach is upset and wants to talk about something with Tina or the children, he feels entitled to discuss it and lecture about it as long and thoroughly as he desires. He expects Tina and the children to listen without interrupting and without leaving. He also gets angry if they are not very attentive.

These are patterns of emotional and verbal abuse and control. It would be wise for Tina to seek help from a counselor or a minister. Often, individuals like Zach don't want any family members talking to anyone outside of the family. However, it is wise and appropriate to do so.

PUT ASIDE ASSUMPTIONS AND INNUENDOES

Communication should be authentic, without innuendos or hidden messages. Marriage partners and family members should not have to guess what is said. Eliminate land mines that need to be avoided or eggshells to walk around. Clarity and transparency are essential and honest.

For healthier marriage and family communication, avoid assumptions. Assuming leads to frustrating confusion. Ask questions to clarify. Give full information and answers. Tell everything pertinent. State all the what, when, where, who, and why facts. Be proactive to share freely.

Communicate clearly, check out everything with each other, and listen fully. Clarify to make sure everyone knows all the same facts, understands the feelings, and then works together for decisions and compromises. Communication is shared information based on all perspectives.

Everyone responds better with clarity and calmness. State what you want to express. Lower negative emotions. Respectfully share facts and feelings. Allow other participants to share what they want to also. Do not let strong opinions and emotions dictate the conversation flow.

The real issues get lost and feelings are difficult when communication is not clear and complete. Keep the issues in focus. Pause and let the other person's thoughts, ideas, and opinions be voiced. As you listen, anticipate that each perspective will be different. That is all right. Listen to each other.

Tony and Susan

Tony works hard and is the provider for the family. He views providing as his job and takes it seriously. It was his hope that Susan would not have to go to work, and she likes being home with their children.

However, for the last few years the budget has become increasingly tight. Tony is feeling overloaded and thinks that Susan may need to get a job. He has mentioned it several times, but she ignores him or says she is too busy. They need to discuss both of their perspectives.

Since the children are all in school, Tony knows Susan spends a lot of time on Facebook or watching TV. Tony has begun using sarcasm about how hard he works and how little Susan does. He needs to apologize for that and be clear about the financial needs.

Susan needs to be willing to discuss a budget and all about their finances. They need to listen to both of their concerns and assess the financial needs of the family. Susan may need to be open to the possibility of her getting at least a part-time job at home.

Communication should be respectful and considerate. The healthiest and happiest marriages are those that proactively communicate and talk through all kinds of things. Positive communication in marriage leads to a greater sense of closeness and satisfaction in the whole relationship.

SAY IT COMPLETELY AND CLEARLY

Clear and complete communication is a key to positive relationships. When communication is ambiguous or muddled, it causes mix-ups and hinders trust. A common problem in marriages is limited conversation and not enough clear content shared. Give the complete information, facts, etc.

Spouses need to communicate about everything: thoughts, feelings, ideas, plans, concerns, joys, hopes, and dreams. Couples can become halfhearted about discussing all necessary aspects of their marriage thoroughly enough. Be intentional to have purposeful and direct conversations.

When one spouse wants to talk about an issue, be open and honest about the desire to discuss it. Give each other a topic "heads-up" and set an agreed time to converse. State your views and desires. Be clear. Don't communicate with ambiguities, vague phrases, or cloaked messages.

Clear communication includes making plans and decisions in unity as a couple. Activities and schedules need to be processed thoroughly and agreed on together before talking with anyone else. Excluding each other causes a spouse to feel marginalized and disregarded.

Minimizing a spouse breaks the trust and causes feelings of being manipulated. The spouse is the most important person and the marriage the priority relationship. Both spouses need to give focused and dedicated attention to subjects discussed. Share thoughts and preferences. Listen to each other's views.

Sonya and Alfred

Sonya and Alfred are disconnected in their communication and feel ignored by each other. Neither one feels validated and informed. Sonya plans trips with girlfriends and only tells Alfred when she is about to pack. She feels he is too busy and bored with the details.

Alfred makes financial decisions without discussing them with Sonya. She finds out when she sees large transfers from the accounts. Alfred thinks he has the mathematical mind and should oversee the finances. Both feel like they get overlooked in communication.

Often with couples, a spouse mistakenly thinks the other spouse knows or should know thoughts and ideas that have not been communicated. He or she may assume the other knows what to buy for a birthday present or where to plan a vacation as a surprise.

This is explained with, "If you love me you should know." Assuming one can read minds is impossible and unfair. No matter how much you love each other or how long you have been married, you cannot read each other's minds or know what the other is feeling unless it is stated.

You may know your spouse's inclinations and habits, but you cannot know their thoughts and emotions unless they tell you. If you need specifics, ask them to explain the information you are wondering about.

Laura and George

Laura likes surprises and believes the myth that a husband should be able to read his wife's mind. She tries to make George figure out what she wants for birthdays and special occasions. He asks her, but she tells him to guess. He tries, but inevitably gets it wrong and misses the mark. She is increasingly disappointed, and he is weary of failing and wants to give up.

Laura is not loving to George when this is her standard or expectation. She should tell him honestly and openly her desires. She should be thankful that he is a loving husband who wants to celebrate her on special occasions. He can also continue to listen to her random expressed preferences throughout the year as well as ask her to know for sure.

Put thoughts and feelings into words, or your spouse will not know. Be committed to verbalizing your desires. They are important and worth being disclosed. Only then can spouses fully understand each other. It is thoughtful and helpful for you to be open and honest about your preferences.

Presume that your spouse wants to honor you and please you, but it is difficult if he or she has not been given necessary information. Don't make your spouse imagine what you want or need. Verbalize these things in kind and understandable ways.

Listen to your spouse's heart and gently respond to needs and desires. Be attentive and sacrificial. Do not be dismissive of what is requested. Don't minimize what your spouse tells you. God blesses marriages when each spouse cares for one another and is responsive to the other.

Be sure that you are not using your personal interests and ideas disguised as caring for your spouse. For example, a husband should not give gifts to his wife to only further his personal hobbies and interests. That indicates that he is loving himself more than her. She will feel disregarded and unloved.

Beth and Stan

Beth and Stan have been married for eight years. They generally have participated in separate hobbies. Through the years, Beth has suggested they develop some interests together and mentioned some options. However, none have developed.

Stan continues to only pursue his activities and buy her

gifts such as fishing poles and hunting gear, hoping she will do his activities. She feels snubbed and unimportant to him. They need to discuss both of their perspectives and preferences and seek some compromise.

APPROPRIATE PACING

> Be devoted to one another in brotherly love.
> Honor one another above yourselves.
> (Romans 12:10)

Another aspect of good communication is that of pacing our conversations. There is a normal rhythm to dialogue. This includes each having the opportunity to participate, share their point of view, listen to each other, and be heard and respected by all involved.

Pacing includes a flow with the up and down and back and forth in conversation. Pacing keeps people engaged, interested, and participating. Pacing helps regulate the speed of the conversation—not too fast or too slow.

Conversations that drag too much make it difficult for the members to stay interested. If the conversation is too fast, it may be difficult for listeners to keep up. Be aware of the course and rhythm of discussions. Make adjustments for other participants.

Pacing helps communication feel fair and appealing to all. Pacing is important in single conversations and discussions with several people. It is one of the ways we learn how a person expresses things and responds. How a person paces shows thoughtfulness to others.

Pacing is also a way to deliberately bring someone into the

conversation by slowing down and allowing them to enter into the verbal process. It is similar to a metaphor of walking along and then someone else joining to walk alongside. Slowing down the discussion to slip someone in, and then picking up the flow to finish the exchange is a good method.

Pacing in communication is a good tool to know when and how to include others in the interaction. One can slow down to emphasize a point or speed up to energize the conversation. Be aware of how other participants are tracking with you.

Be cautious that you don't leave anyone out as you are speaking or that you don't run over someone who is talking. Often in marriages, one spouse is talkative while the other is quieter. It is important for the talkative spouse to slow down and not push out the other spouse.

Equally, the quiet spouse needs to be willing to engage and express more. Step up and take initiative to share things. Being encouraged to talk is a sweet invitation. Accept it and communicate with energy and interest.

Donald and Michelle

Donald is a big talker and an extrovert. Michelle is quiet and reserved. Donald talks a lot in the marriage and does not notice when Michelle tries to speak up about her thoughts and feelings. Without listening, he runs over her in the conversations, gets ahead of her, interrupts, and does not pay attention to what she says.

Recently, when with another couple, Donald heard Michelle say some things that made him realize how hurt she feels when he doesn't listen and care about her feelings. Donald went home that night and apologized to Michelle.

He is trying hard to slow down and give her more opportunity to speak. She is trying to gain confidence in discussions. She is feeling more loved and speaking up more. He is listening and learning wonderful things about his sweet wife.

5

WORDS THAT BUILD UP

Do not let any unwholesome talk come out of
your mouths,
but only what is helpful for building others up according to their needs,
that it may benefit those who listen.
—Ephesians 4:29

MORE THAN FORTY years ago, as a young married woman, I went to a church to hear a popular speaker. In a church service before the conference began, the speaker spoke to a group of young children. She read to them Ephesians 4:29. Then she asked, "What are words?" A little girl about six years old thought a moment, raised her hand, and said, "Silver packages wrapped in blue bows."

I gasped at the wealth of wisdom in what she said. Clearly,

someone had taught her that words are gifts we give. As she thought about the prettiest gift she could imagine, she said silver packages with blue bows. For these forty-plus years, I have had a small silver package wrapped up with a blue bow hanging on our refrigerator, reminding me that my words should be like presents to give to those around me.

Ephesians 4:29 has several important qualifiers that our words should have. First, our words should always be wholesome. They should be helpful for building others up according to their needs, and they should benefit those who listen.

These instructions would not be in the Bible if they were for the calm times, when it is easy for nice words to flow out of our mouths. We don't need biblical instruction for that because we can do that in our own human strength.

Rather, this verse is a commandment especially for the difficult times, when being kind and gracious is the last thing we want to do. It is for when we want to be reactionary and justify saying whatever we are feeling.

This commandment is for times when relationships are strained, pride is bristled, emotions are tense, feelings are wounded, and we don't want to talk wholesomely. It is at these especially relevant times that we have to be most careful to not respond based on our emotions.

We can't choose if and when we want to apply this biblical verse. It is a mandate to treat people in right and kind ways at all times. It is powerful in shaping loving, grace-filled communications that build others up.

Remember times when someone said something that impacted you in a positive way? Do you likewise remember times when words sliced your heart? If this happened at an important time in your life, or by a significant person to you, you may experience the lasting influence of those words in your heart.

In the same way, your words can affect others for good or harm. Make a life commitment that your words will be wholesome to encourage people. Positive words can be life-changing and empowering in many ways. Let your words be gifts to others to bless them, give hope and strength, and point them to Christ.

AFFIRMATION, PRAISE, AND ENCOURAGEMENT

Affirmation and encouragement are very powerful in the life of every person. Affirmations are strong and gracious words that address the good qualities of a person. Affirmation recognizes people for positive actions, attitudes, and characteristics. It is a meaningful gift we can give to others to lift them up.

Affirmation includes seeing potential, appreciating a good job, acknowledging effort, and recognizing noble traits. Affirming words encourage individuals to keep on trying and continue doing what is right. Words of recognition motivate one to persevere and stay the course.

> An anxious heart weighs a man down, but a kind word cheers him up.
>
> (Proverbs 12:25)

Genuine praise and encouragement for others cost us nothing but give priceless positive regard for those who receive it. In whatever method it is communicated, affirmation energizes and strengthens those who accept it, and leaves indelible messages in the hearts of the beneficiaries. Be known as an encourager.

The Bible instructs all of us to be generous in our words

of praise and acknowledgment. Look for ways to regularly give this gift. Share it with people who need it and deserve it. If you want to give individuals a good day, or to impact their life, affirm and praise them.

Focus on being loving when you talk to your spouse and family members. This takes commitment because it may not always match your emotions in the moment. Regular times of kindness, validation, and understanding allow for other times of correction to be received more easily.

Talk favorably about your spouse to other people. If you brag on your spouse when he or she is not around, recount it later. Share your praise and how proud you are. Express encouragement for positive qualities that are noteworthy regarding their heart, character, personal strengths, and special abilities. It will be a blessing to your spouse.

Paul and Cindy

Paul and Cindy are often in conflict about several issues. Paul responds with frustration and impatience and says unkind things to Cindy. He also says unkind things about her to others. He does not see his own faults and selfish actions.

Cindy feels hurt and disrespected. She knows they need to address issues but is discouraged because Paul's words are so crushing. He likes for her to talk positively about him to others, though he is quick to be critical and condescending about her. Paul is hurting Cindy and breaking her trust. She does not want to open up about anything.

APPRECIATION AND THANKSGIVING

Appreciation invigorates a person. Express it for thoughtful actions, jobs well done, efforts given, and positive traits. It says, "I noticed" and "Your contributions are valuable." Think of new and different ways to say thank you. Capitalize on them daily for your spouse and family members.

Express this appreciation regularly through words, gifts, actions, and affection. No need to wait for holidays and special occasions. In fact, sometimes the unexpected times are received with even greater delight and enjoyment.

Every person in your family needs and deserves appreciation expressed to them, even when they are moving toward what is right and are still in the process. Tell them how much you love them and are thankful for them. Be mindful of the many special qualities that you value in these individuals.

Remember your love for your children from the moment God gave them to you. Think of how thankful you are for your family members, and how much they mean to you. Deeply appreciate them. Express this to them. Pursue them in conversation. Catch up often.

Ask about your loved one's day, staying current with events and emotions. Ask how you can pray for them. Follow up to pray and later ask them for updates. It will communicate to them that you are serious about praying for them.

Aaron and Nelda

Aaron and Nelda loved each other but had frequent arguments. Usually the conflicts did not get completely resolved and left residual heartache and dismay. Then one day Aaron humbly and genuinely apologized, promised to change, and asked Nelda to forgive him.

He chose to become more thankful for Nelda and express appreciation for her regularly. Aaron took steps to prove his words and change his wrong ways. Nelda asked him to forgive her also for things she had done and said that were not loving.

Since then, both are trying to affirm the good traits in each other. Treating each other with kindness and appreciation has caused the arguments to be fewer and calmer. They thank each other for serving and for all they do to bless and benefit the marriage.

COMMITMENT AND SERVICE

Remember how you fell in love with your spouse? You tenderly expressed your love and proclaimed your commitment. This love is not based on the events of the day, your spouse's behavior, or your emotions. It is a foundational promise that should remain steadfast.

There may be times when your spouse doesn't handle things appropriately and may disappoint and hurt you. That comes with our humanity. Address the issues appropriately and lovingly. Do not overlook the offenses, but don't chastise your spouse either.

Express your love and commitment. Look at the positive and be encouraging. Invest in the relationship by doing actions to show you cherish your spouse. Affirm your spouse's great traits. Recommit your love in tender and meaningful ways daily.

Listen to your spouse's feelings and burdens when he or she is sharing about heavy responsibilities, uncertainties, and concerns. Ask, "How can I lighten your load today? How can I pray for you?" Then make it a priority to follow up and do what your spouse suggests and requests.

Show sacrificial love by serving your spouse. Look for ways to do more to help with the family, chores, and maintenance around the home. Express your thankfulness and appreciation for all your spouse does. Healthy marriages consistently help each other and affirm one another.

Helen and Mark

Helen had volunteered to help with the church Thanksgiving banquet. On the day of the banquet, several of her helpers were sick or had to cancel. She called others to help, without success. She called Mark upset and sad. Mark had been out of town all week busy with big projects.

Shortly after Mark arrived home late that afternoon, he surprised Helen when he came to the church with an apron in hand. Though he was planning to care for the children, he had called his mom to watch the children so he could help Helen. She felt deeply loved and very thankful for his willingness and service.

GENTLENESS AND SELF-CONTROL

Important aspects of communication are gentleness and self-control. How we say something is as important as what we say. Communicating with a gentle attitude and a calmness gives the other person a feeling of safety and acceptance.

Gentleness is respectful. Recognizing the importance of lowering the intensity in discussions and exhibiting self-control give a sense of peace and calmness. Self-control regulates our emotions and maintains a kinder approach.

> But the fruit of the Spirit is love, joy, peace, patience,
> kindness, goodness, faithfulness, gentleness, and self-control.
> Against such things there is no law.
> (Galatians 5:22-23)

This verse includes nine relational characteristics that describe the fruit of the Holy Spirit. They are impossible to replicate genuinely apart from the Holy Spirit. We need to live surrendered to the Holy Spirit in our life. As believers we belong to God and not to self. Let God's Spirit rule in your heart.

The Holy Spirit helps us **love** when others are not being lovable or loving. It gives **joy** in the midst of life's turmoil, brings **peace** in conflicts, gives **patience** when others are impatient, enables **kindness** when others are mean, shows **goodness** in the face of evil and **faithfulness** when you want to give up. It exhibits **gentleness** when others are harsh and provides **self-control** when you are tempted to be reactionary.

We cannot let destructive human feelings trip us up. We all struggle with emotions when angry or frustrated. But we must not allow our emotions to cause us to sin against others. These verses teach us to let God's Spirit guide how we respond in all circumstances.

You may be the only person in a conflict who is trying to do what is right. Pause. Pray. The Lord will help you know what is appropriate to do and how to communicate in the best way. Choose your words carefully. Be known as a person of kindness and gentleness even when emotions are challenging.

> Do to others as you would have them do to you.
> (Luke 6:31)

A noteworthy guideline whenever you have to discuss difficult things is often called the Golden Rule. It means to treat others in the same way that we would want them to treat us in reverse. Our words and actions should always be a blessing and an encouragement to those who are the recipients.

Everything can and should be discussed in marriage. This means speaking with respect and compassion no matter what the topic, circumstances, or emotions are. I have heard people say that speaking the truth is love. That is not exactly what the verse below says. Actually, the emphasis is on speaking the truth in a loving way.

> Instead, speaking the truth in love, we will in all things grow up
> into him who is the Head, that is, Christ.
> (Ephesians 4:15)

Be cautious and careful with any communication that is painful, discouraging, or difficult. Caring about the feelings of others is thoughtful, kind, and respectful. The method, timing, and content are all important in communication.

When concerns need to be addressed, the "sandwich method" is a good guideline. As in a sandwich, the soft, good bread is on both sides and the meat is in the middle. Begin the confronting conversation with affirmation and appreciation (soft and good). Then discuss the "meat," of the issue, being as concise as possible. End the conversation with more kind affirmation.

KINDNESS AND COMPASSION

Other important aspects of communication are kindness and compassion. Compassion gives a feeling of being understood and valued. Kind conversations show a gentleness that gives respect. That produces a sense of acceptance and openness.

Humble yourself and recognize when you have wrongdoings and shortcomings. Lower your pride to see the other person's perspective. Validate your spouse's viewpoints and emotions. You both can have important feelings and information from different angles. Seek to find common ground.

> Therefore, as God's chosen people, holy and dearly loved, clothe yourselves with
> compassion, kindness, humility, gentleness, and patience.
> (Colossians 3:12)

This verse is a picture of wrapping oneself in compassion, kindness, humility, gentleness, and patience. Imagine if those characteristics were so strong in our lives that people seldom remembered what we were wearing, but instead remembered how they felt cared for and treated with gentleness and patience in our presence.

Frances was known in her family and in all of her relationships for her steady emotions and kind communication. She was gentle in how she treated people and took time to engage with people graciously in conversation. As a result, people enjoyed being with her and sought her friendship.

GRACE, MERCY, AND HOPE

"God loves you." "God has a plan for your life." "He will help you." "God will bring good from this." "God will make us strong through this." "God will never leave us." These statements summarize some promises from the Bible. Often the most important things we can say to our spouse and family member we love so much are reminders of God's love and goodness.

These words of hope help to strengthen our faith in God. God's love changes our life completely. He empowers us to live a life of love with others. He also guides us to treat others with respect. God gives joy, hope, and strength when we walk with faith in Him.

Grace-filled communication helps the listener feel loved and accepted. Encouraging words invite others to continue growing to become a better person. These positive interactions enrich relationships and build up individuals.

Give the benefit of the doubt and assume the best about your spouse. Look for ways to rebuild the trust if it is shaky. Be intentional about strengthening accountability. State the commitments to your spouse and apply them as promised.

When your spouse or family member sins against you, confesses that wrongdoing, apologizes and promises to repent and change, allow for that opportunity. That is how grace and mercy can be shown.

Josh and Lilly

Josh and Lilly had been married for five years. Lilly looked at the finances and realized that Josh had been moving large amounts of money without telling her. He denied everything when she confronted him. Later, he confessed that he had gotten into some online gambling.

She was angry, disappointed, and fearful because their accounts were very low. She asked him to get a second job to earn back some of the deficits and to get into a recovery program. He agreed and did both. To his surprise, Lilly found an additional part-time job to help.

He asked, "Why are you getting a second job? I was the one who squandered our money." She responded, "Because I love you and I forgive you. I can see in you a changed heart. I want to encourage you." He was amazed at her mercy and grace toward him. He repented completely and changed.

6

CONNECTING IN CONFLICTS

> Therefore, if you are offering your gift at the altar and there remember
> that your brother has something against you, leave your gift there in front of the altar.
> First go and be reconciled to your brother; then come and offer your gift.
> —Matthew 5:23-24

CAUSES OF CONFLICTS

JESUS TAUGHT THAT when a relationship is hurting, each person involved should take the initiative to go talk with the other one and seek to reconcile. We should try to talk in a timely way without much delay. My take on Matthew 5:23-24 is "don't wait on the other person, and don't wait around."

People are unique and see things differently. Everyone experiences life from one view…his own. Also, human nature is sinful and self-focused. This means that a selfish perspective is common and a root cause for conflicts.

Conflicts develop when individuals' desires and opinions collide. Human hearts can quickly become frustrated, angry, and defensive. This can happen in any relationship rapidly. The emotions rise as quickly as the differences appear.

Caring more about the other person's interests does not come easily. People overvalue their personal opinions and preferences. Life is viewed through the lens of how things impact us. Changing that lens happens when we attribute value to the other person.

> Do nothing out of selfish ambition or vain conceit, but in humility consider others
> better than yourselves. Each of you should look
> not only to your own interests, but also
> to the interests of others. Your attitude should be
> the same as that of Christ Jesus.
> (Philippians 2:3-5)

Through every conflict, some of the most important words to say to your spouse at different times are "I love you and I am committed to you." This resets the focus back on how precious your spouse is and your promises to the marriage. It also empowers for resolving the conflicts.

TYPICAL REACTIONS TO CONFLICTS

> My dear brothers, take note of this: Everyone should be quick to listen,
> slow to speak and slow to become angry, for man's anger
> does not bring about the righteous life that God desires.
>
> (James 1:19-20)

These verses contain three powerful instructions that can calm a conflict. Be **quick to listen** and hear the other person first. Be **slow to speak** by taking time to think before you speak. Be **slow to become angry.** Keep emotions and intensity calm.

Marriage is the primary and closest relationship. Spouses share the nearest physical spaces and interface in every part of life. Your spouse should be the person you love more than anyone else. Yet arguments with your spouse can be the most difficult.

Spouses can be conversing kindly, then oops…something is said that quickly bristles the emotions of the other one. Suddenly you feel like adversaries instead of teammates. You look at your spouse and think, *What happened to my loving spouse who was just here?*

Couples can become conflicted, impatient, and self-focused. Deep emotions awaken. Intensity can escalate, and extreme statements may be made. Behaviors can get out of control. The more a spouse determines to fight for personal desires, the more entrenched the conflict can become.

Couples need to set guidelines for how conflicts will be

managed. The best time to commit to these guidelines is before disagreements arise. Your willingness to make these promises is based on your love for one another and the desire for a kind and respectful marriage.

In arguments, agreements can be quickly cast aside in the flurry of selfish reactions. Emotions can hijack you, blinding your ability to reset the incident in a good way. Hurt feelings and sadness will ensue. Pause, gain self-control, and remember how much you love your spouse.

Gina and Philip

Gina asked Philip if he would stay home with their young children while she went to a PTA meeting with Martha, the PTA president. He agreed. As it turned out, the meeting ran long. Gina texted Philip, explaining and apologizing that they could not leave because Martha was presiding. She felt bad that it was running late.

When she arrived home, Gina apologized again, but Philip was impatient and angry. He talked harshly to her even though being late was not her fault. His lack of kindness and understanding hurt Gina's feelings and made her feel disrespected.

BETTER RESPONSES

> In your anger do not sin.
>
> (Ephesians 4:26)

Marriage is a treasure and deserves loving care. Disrespectful conflicts hurt a marriage. There is much at stake and the risks are high. When arguments occur, couples need to intentionally make positive, selfless, and loving choices for greater marital well-being.

Remember past conflicts with your spouse. How could things have been handled differently to refocus on the importance of the marriage? Determine ways for calmer heads to prevail next time to help each spouse voice feelings with lower intensity.

Organize the Issues

In a conflict, state the issues. Ask for a time-out for each to write down bullet points of issues and concerns. This will organize your thoughts and yield a workable list. Talk through problems one at a time. Issues and concerns are difficult but need to be discussed. They can become more critical if avoided.

Lower the Volume

> A gentle answer turns away wrath, but a harsh word stirs up anger.
>
> (Proverbs 15:1)

This verse teaches that we should talk in a calm, kind voice tone even when we are upset. This takes commitment. As anger increases, usually the volume increases also. Lowering the volume is essential. Sit down. Lower your body to lower the volume. The most positive level for hearing each other and working out problems is a quiet, normal voice tone. Each raised level becomes less productive.

Listen to Each Other

Listen carefully to each other. Take turns speaking. Listen to your spouse without pondering what you want to say. Seek to understand your spouse's position as much as you want your spouse to understand yours. Ask questions to clarify. Give your spouse a chance to answer. Be succinct, knowing your spouse wants to share thoughts also.

Give Your Attention

During important discussions, limit distractions and interruptions. Put away devices, phones, newspapers, and other things. This helps to maintain the priority of the relationship. Focus on your spouse. Give your spouse your undivided attention because her/his thoughts and feelings are important to you.

Calm Your Emotions

Cool down your emotions. Take deep breaths. Oxygen is important. Sit down to see each other eye to eye for productive conversation. Talk kindly and graciously. Remember that you love this person you are in conflict with. Express your love.

State the Facts

Explain the problem and your perspective. Be honest about the facts. When untrue accusations are made toward you, correct them respectfully. Do not make assumptions regarding your spouse's thoughts or feelings. Be proactive and discuss issues early and calmly. Seek a compromise or new solution. It may not be your most desired answer. That is alright.

Avoid Self-Focus

Do not be defensive, sensitive, and negative. Do not become dramatic. Do not allow your feelings to be hurt easily. Give more concern for your spouse's feelings than your own. See things from your spouse's perspective. Do not make general, broad deflecting accusations. Do not make patronizing or condescending statements. Do not let emotions drive you.

Pace Yourself

Agree on a time to talk. Use a timer to share time equally. Slow down the emotions. Take breaks as needed. Stay calm. Focus on listening to each other while seeking an agreement or compromise. Practice self-control. Do not let intensity get ahead of you. Get help from an objective third person if the conflict cannot be resolved in a reasonable time.

DIFFERENT APPROACHES TO CONFLICT

Carla and Matthew

Carla and Matthew struggle in arguments and quickly become upset. Matthew is easily angered and wants to resolve everything immediately. Carla is quieter and needs time to process through things and discuss them later.

That frustrates Matthew, who believes Carla avoids conflicts and is not willing to solve problems. Carla feels like Matthew does not care about her feelings and wants his way.

He follows her around the house trying to force her to talk. She gets more upset and can't stop crying.

It is common for married couples to have one spouse who wants to resolve conflicts as soon as possible and the other spouse wants to calm down, consider things before trying to resolve issues.

The first one pushes toward the other one, insisting, "We need to talk right now." This shuts the quiet spouse down even more and runs over her or him emotionally. The second one usually pulls inward and away to sort out thoughts and feelings. This makes the other spouse feel ignored and fearful of avoidance.

It is good to resolve conflicts in a timely way, and it is also good to take time to bring emotions under control and to evaluate our words carefully. The one who wants to resolve things quickly needs to slow down, be loving, and patiently say, "I know you need some time. When can we talk?"

The reserved spouse knows that conflict resolution needs discussion and that the other spouse wants to work through issues as soon as possible. The request for a break should be for a short time and should also include stating a time to come back and talk. Then come together at the agreed time to seek to resolve the conflicts.

During the break, each should pray. Ask God to help you resolve this together in a good way. Write down issues and thoughts to discuss. "Move to the middle" in the relationship by choosing to act in love graciously to understand the other's perspective.

Sometimes a spouse demands to resolve issues quickly, quoting Ephesians 4:26 about not letting the sun go down on your anger. That verse does not mean that issues have to be resolved before midnight or that "no one sleeps till we work this out."

This verse teaches that resolving conflicts is a priority in relationships. Problems should be worked out as soon as possible. There needs to be a commitment to process disagreements thoroughly, carefully, and in a timely manner. Actually, many arguments in marriage happen after the sun has already gone down.

Conflicts usually occur at inconvenient times. If you need to delay the talking time, plan to discuss things at least by the next day if possible. Do not let conflicts linger unresolved. They can develop relational scar tissue that brings less flexibility and more pain. Seek help sooner rather than later.

INTENSITY, TONE, AND VOLUME

Important aspects of communication and conflict resolution are the *intensity, tone,* and *volume*. Any one of these can quickly sabotage communication and lead it down a difficult path. Careful attention must be given to these three characteristics so that the conversation can stay positive.

The **intensity** is the strength of the emotional undertones of the speaker. Lower intensity can provide openness. Higher intensity feels confrontational. Simply put, intensity shows how tense the conversation is. Necessary emotional adjustments help everyone.

Reducing tense reactions lowers the other person's defenses. Regardless of what the sentiments are, it is best to calm down and speak normally. Higher tensions repel others and cause guardedness. They also result in the whole relationship feeling negative or broken.

The second component is **tone**. Tone depicts the permeating tenor, mood, or attitude of the speaker. The tone of the conversation has to do with the sound of the communicator's voice. The tone is a descriptor that defines the conversation apart from the words spoken.

Taking the frustration out of your voice enhances conflict resolution. Tone reveals the softness or harshness of the speaker. It is noticed if one's voice has a "sharp edge" to it. When a person is speaking briskly, it may come across to the listener as frustrated or annoyed.

The third characteristic is **volume**. Volume determines how loudly or softly a speaker is speaking. High volume causes the conversation to be less productive and difficult to hear clearly. It becomes negative and ending in frustration and disconnection. Lower volume is considerate and quieting.

No one likes to be talked to in a harsh or abrasive voice. A loud voice may project authority but devalues the listeners. Typically, high volume receives two responses from those listening. It causes elevated volume from the other person, or it produces a response of silence and distancing.

When the volume is notched up even one level, discourse becomes less effective. The next level becomes harmful and destructive. There should be great intent to decompress and lower the volume as soon as possible.

Don't wait on the other person to calm down. Don't try to "dish it back." Lower your own intensity and say, "Please, time out. Let's lower the volume. I love you and I don't want to hurt you with my words or tone."

COP-OUTS, CUTOFFS, AND TIME-OUTS

It is important to look for ways to resolve conflicts. Decompressing the tension is also important. However, there are some methods that are detrimental and are not helpful or recommended. A variety of actions may include **cop-outs, cut-offs** or **time-outs**.

Cop-outs are an effort to end the conversation by separation and avoidance. These reduce accountability and elevate rejection and abandonment. In explosive conversation, one partner may scream, "I'm out of here!" The door slams. And the car revs off.

The other spouse is left wondering if and when he or she will return. Cop-outs are open-ended, hurtful, and distressing. They are only for the benefit of the exiting spouse. They break the trust and leave lingering residual feelings of disregard. Cop-outs seek to project control and or manipulation.

Cop-outs are refusing to discuss issues and responding with neglect and detachment. They are contrary to marriage commitments, are selfish, destructive and lack concern for the spouse. Cop-outs may give the implementer a feeling of power and influence, but they cause uncertainty and apprehension in the remaining spouse.

Bradley and Shannon

Bradley angrily leaves the house when he and Shannon have a fight. He does not tell her where he is going, what he will be doing, or when he will be back. He leaves her at home alone with their young baby and no other car. There have been numerous times that Shannon is left sobbing and fearful.

Her parents live out of town. She doesn't know many people there and wonders how much longer she can endure this.

Bradley refuses to go to counseling. She has made a commitment that tomorrow she is calling the lady who leads her Bible study class. She needs help.

Cutoffs are emotional "shut-outs." They occur when a spouse or family member cuts off a relationship. Cutoffs block a spouse from any inroad or contact point to interact. Cutoffs make a person feel powerless in the relationship. They leave a person feeling discarded and worthless.

Cutoffs are prideful and selfish. They declare, "I am not going to talk to you, and I am not going to have a relationship with you." Cutoffs are punitive and sever connection. They are usually implemented recklessly by dominance and control. Cutoffs are the silent treatment.

If you face adverse reactions when you express your opinions, needs, or desires, protect yourself and do not say much. If you are in a marriage where you do not feel emotionally or physically safe, seek outside help from a minister or a biblical counselor.

The healthiest of these methods of handling conflicts is seen in the appropriate use of **time-outs.** Time-outs are intentional, designated periods of time to calm down emotional intensity. This helps to recalibrate the focus to enable having a discussion in a fair and respectful way.

This might look like a spouse saying, "I need to catch my breath and have a moment to pause." "I need to calm down and pray." "I love you. I don't want to hurt you. I need to pause for a few minutes." Time-outs feel considerate to each person.

Conversations can benefit from a pause to take a few deep breaths. Inhale…exhale. Inhale…exhale. Oxygen to the brain is not overrated. It produces clearer thinking and calmer emotions. If a little more time is needed, perhaps something like,

"May we pause for a glass of lemonade or a quick snack?" Remember, even difficult conversations can be discussed on a normal voice level.

If your spouse asks for a time-out, honor their request, and choose the least amount of time as possible. For example, "May we talk after dinner?" or "Can we talk tomorrow when I get home from my trip?" The one who is asking for a time-out is also responsible for naming a time back in to connect. Be faithful to follow up without making your spouse ask.

Let your spouse and family member know that "even though we are disagreeing about something, you are important to me. I want us to resolve our conflicts." Thoughtful consideration to show you desire to get back in sync with each other is loving and assuring.

Lucy and Ralph

Lucy and Ralph stay very conflicted in their marriage. Disagreements do not get resolved. Lucy avoids talking about important topics and shuts down, refusing to talk for days.

Ralph tries to approach conversations kindly and gently, but Lucy is easily offended. She ignores him as if he is invisible. He does not know how to help them move forward. A third neutral person who is wise and godly is needed.

CAUTIONS AND CONCLUSIONS IN CONFLICT RESOLUTION

In your marriage do not drive away angry. With upset feelings, driving safely is difficult. Do not use mindless driving to process your emotions. Many people have driven aimlessly, only to later realize they were far from home or in an unfamiliar place because they were not paying attention to their driving.

If you need a break, let your spouse and family members know that you just need a few minutes to calm your thoughts and emotions. State where you will be and when you plan to return. Come back soon to continue talking and working toward a relational resolution. Stay nearby and do a positive physical activity such as playing basketball on the driveway, walking around the block, or working in the yard.

Going to the gym may not be the best option in conflicts. When you are upset, you are more prone to physical injuries as you may overexert to "let off steam." Also, your emotions may be more vulnerable, and temptations can happen easily. Guard your heart to protect your marriage.

When you experience conflicts in your marriage, recognize that you and your spouse are still on the same team instead of opponents. Work together toward creative compromises and solutions. Remember the value of your marriage. Then you will have fewer regrets in the future.

When conflicts have been resolved, ask each other some questions. "Do you have anything else you want to say?" "Is there anything I need to do?" "What can I do better next time in a conflict so that you feel loved?" Make sure that each spouse is heard and respected. Make positive decisions for future conflicts and follow through in coming times.

Express love, allegiance, and thanksgiving for your spouse. Focus on the positive traits and agree to love more selflessly in your marriage. Pray together, confessing and asking for God's healing and restoration in your marriage. Pray for yourself and for your spouse. Ask God to bless your marriage. Move forward with greater commitments for the strengthening of your marriage.

> Not that I have already obtained all this, or have
> already been made perfect,
> but I press on to take hold of that for which
> Christ Jesus took hold of me.
> Brothers, I do not consider myself yet to have
> taken hold of it.
> But one thing I do: Forgetting what is behind and
> straining toward what is ahead,
> I press on toward the goal to win the prize for
> which
> God has called me heavenward in Christ Jesus.
> (Philippians 3:12-14)

7

DESTRUCTIVE COMMUNICATION

The good man brings good things out of the good stored up in him,
and the evil man brings evil things out of the evil stored up in him.
But I tell you that men will have to give account on the day of judgment
for every careless word they have spoken. For by your words
you will be acquitted, and by your words you will be condemned.
—Matthew 12:35-37

IT IS VERY important to realize what destructive communications are and how they can negatively impact your loved ones.

You may have grown up with some of these patterns and then incorporated them into your adult life, marriage, and family. However, these must be addressed and changed.

Through Jesus Christ, there is hope for renewal. The Bible gives help and instructions for how we should communicate with and relate to others. The Holy Spirit empowers the believer to have motivation and strength for positive growth.

Charles and His Family

Charles came home from work, kicking young Anna's bike on the front porch, cursing and calling to her, "Why did you leave your bike on the porch?" As he came through the front door, he yelled unkind names to his son Danny about parking the car crooked on the driveway. Then he was angry and mean with Connie, his wife, because dinner wasn't quite ready.

The family all sat down for dinner, but no one felt like talking except Charles. After dinner, everyone just wanted to do their own thing alone in separate bedrooms. The next morning, Charles was up early, whistling and wearing an apron. He called up the stairs, "Wake up, everyone, and hurry down. I've made pancakes!"

However, they didn't really want his pancakes. They would much rather have a sincere apology for his anger, bad language, name calling, and hurtful comments from the night before. Charles is oblivious to the pain and heartbreak he pours out on his family from his own harsh selfishness and destructive communication. There are many corrections he needs to make.

Destructive communication is very harmful with lasting painful results. Abusive, unkind, or disrespectful words can greatly harm someone mentally, emotionally, relationally, and spiritually. Hurtful communication breaks hearts and crushes spirits.

Destructive communication reflects the heart of the speaker. Harsh discourses and mean-spirited conversations reveal an arrogant perspective in the speaker. It does not reflect the value or worth of the recipient. God loves every person and gives importance to each one.

Recipients of destructive communication can feel emotionally immobilized. They may feel like change is futile. Those individuals can seek help from ministers, counselors, and friends. Take the initiative to talk with a neutral person who can help you find needed protection and support.

DEROGATORY

Communication that is belittling, condescending, or patronizing is destructive. It tears people down and disregards the significance of each person. Individuals who use destructive communication enjoy a "one-up" position. They may even have a sinful view that the other person deserves it. They are usually in denial and lack concern about their habitual negative speech and the devastation that it causes.

Discounting, putting someone down, or making demeaning comments are characteristics of a person who doesn't attach much priority to other people. The tendency is to minimize the worth of others while elevating one's personal merit. This is self-focused and wrong. Negative communication breaks hearts and crushes spirits.

The lips of the righteous know what is fitting,
but the mouth of the wicked only what is perverse.
(Proverbs 10:32)
He who guards his lips guards his life;
But he who speaks rashly will come to ruin.
(Proverbs 13:3)

Damon and Monica

Damon is being a good husband and father, working two jobs and carrying many responsibilities at work and home. However, Monica continuously belittles him and talks down to him. She minimizes the good job he is doing, while she settles for doing the minimum herself. She says he is just trying to impress others.

Monica talks to Damon like he is not smart and treats him with contempt. She does not acknowledge his accomplishments and is critical of everything he does, as if she could do better. He feels like he does not measure up and that Monica is never pleased.

Justin and Dorothy

Justin vacillates between being nice at times and then saying unkind things at other times. The negative comments blindside Dorothy, hurt deeply, and pull her inward relationally. Justin may give a shallow apology and then want Dorothy to be physically intimate with him right away. Justin thinks that will clear everything up.

He does not understand that emotional closeness and

security need to be present before he can expect Dorothy to want to be physically intimate. If she does not want to have sex then, he says unkind things to her, pushing her away emotionally even more. This is emotionally abusive.

ANGRY WORDS AND EXPRESSIONS

Intense emotions, anger, raging, quick temper, yelling and screaming are all descriptions of sinful communication. They reveal spiritual, relational, and emotional immaturity. Sometimes these may be patterns of negative communication that can also be linked to other out of control areas like extreme selfishness, alcohol use, addictions or financial issues.

These individuals often exhibit extreme destructive communication and reckless emotions. Anytime something happens that is not what they want, they react with severe dysfunctional behaviors, annihilating others in their path. They justify their anger and actions while showing no grace to others.

These prideful selfish people may need to be confronted by people who can defend the persons being mistreated. Generally, these raging people do not listen to correction and minimize their caustic behaviors. They justify and rationalize their words and feel an entitlement to harm others.

> Reckless words pierce like a sword,
> but the tongue of the wise brings healing.
> (Proverbs 12:18)
> Do you see a man who speaks in haste?
> There is more hope for a fool than for them.
> (Proverbs 29:20)

> A fool gives full vent to his anger, but a wise man keeps himself under control.
>
> (Proverbs 29:11)

Blaine and Carmen

Blaine is an angry man. He is often raging at his wife, Carmen, and their sweet children. He yells every day about something. His uncontrolled anger is destroying his marriage and family. Carmen and the children try to stay away from Blaine and his unpredictable wrath.

Blaine seems content only when he is wielding relational control and gratifying personal desires. That is usually when he is in his recliner drinking beer. He is in denial about the negative effects of his anger and his drinking. Blaine's heart is evident by his selfishness and disregard for others. He is blinded to the emotional debris that he leaves behind.

SILENT TREATMENT

A seemingly passive approach to anger is the silent treatment. It actually indicates a great deal of pride. The silent treatment is manipulative and controlling. It is used to withhold communication and closeness until a personal desire is satisfied.

The silent treatment is a method of focusing on self. It withholds interaction and delays resolving the problem. It basically says, "I am not going to be nice to you until I get what I want."

> Get rid of all bitterness, rage and anger,
> brawling and slander, along with every form of malice.
>
> (Ephesians 4:31)

Micah and Nancy

Micah lets his frustration rob his marriage. Micah says he loves Nancy, but he likes his preferences more. He gets aggravated when Nancy is running late, when she asks to buy something, when she wants to have her family over, and when she asks him to help with a chore.

Micah resents serving and acts like everything is an imposition. He fusses, fumes, is impatient, and slams things around. If Micah doesn't get his desires, he stops talking to Nancy for hours or days. He refuses to care about her feelings. His stubborn anger is punitive and sabotaging.

BLAMING, MISCONSTRUING OTHER'S WORDS

Deliberately changing what someone says, blaming everything on someone else, and misconstruing the words of another person are all harmful and unkind. Often in a marriage a spouse will want to talk about issues and express concerns and problems. However, the other person may deflect the responsibility and procrastinate discussions.

The blaming spouse denies and avoids healthy and positive communication. He or she shifts it back to accuse the other spouse. Not giving validity to a spouse's feelings and concerns overlooks one's intrinsic value and worth. This negating behavior minimizes personal accountability and seeks to dump on the spouse.

Not accepting personal involvement for one's own responsibilities and issues is selfish and detrimental. Avoiding confessing and only blaming the other, is wrong. This can cause the other person to become exasperated, want to leave and or shut down. It breaks trust in the marriage.

Another reason a marriage partner can feel disrespected is if the other spouse presumes things or takes things for granted. This can happen in several scenarios: when a spouse does not include the other, does not give notice about issues, or assumes thoughts or beliefs without allowing or asking for the necessary pertinent information.

> A fool takes no pleasure in understanding,
> but delights in airing his own opinions.
>
> (Proverbs 18:2)
>
> Put away perversity from your mouth; keep corrupt talk far from your lips.
>
> (Proverbs 4:24)

Donnie and Chloe

Donnie asks Chloe to talk with him about finances. She refuses and spends money with disregard for their agreed plan. Lately she has written two checks that have bounced. Donnie tries to talk with Chloe about the need to discipline the spending and how to balance the account.

Chloe says the problem is that Donnie doesn't make enough money for the family. She blames him, saying he's stingy. Chloe says that when they married, he told her he wanted to provide for her. She says, "Then I should be able to buy whatever I want."

Martha and Raymond

Martha feels emotionally impoverished by Raymond's dictatorial patterns in their marriage and family. He has rules about everything and wants to control all parts of their life. He scrutinizes whatever she does and regularly criticizes Martha and the children.

Raymond accuses Martha of trying to deliberately go against him. She tells him that is not correct. She has asked Raymond to go to counseling with her, but he refuses. In frustration and dismay she can't stop crying, often wanting time alone. Raymond blames her, saying her crying is the problem. "You just cry all the time."

He says she is emotionally weak and needs to grow up. She tells him that his behavior causes her to feel extremely sad and hopeless. He claims he has done nothing wrong. Raymond discounts his precipitating and controlling demeanor. He also disregards Martha's feelings and desires.

PROFANITY AND NAME CALLING

Profanity and name calling are some of the most abusive forms of destructive communication. These methods of expressing things represent a dark and idolatrous heart. When someone prioritizes self over everyone else, then whenever anything is not exactly what that person wants, there is an assumption that emotions can be expressed in any selfish method chosen.

A verbally abusive person justifies the negative communication and arrogant mindset, minimizes the harmful impact on others, and justifies it with sinful explanations such as "They deserved it." Negative communication is felt as more hurtful by the recipients. The speaker usually refuses to acknowledge the devastation and emotional wreckage left in the wake of the arrogant disregard.

> A man of perverse heart does not prosper; he
> whose tongue is deceitful falls into trouble.
> (Proverbs 17:20)
>
> But now you must rid yourselves of all such things
> as these:
> anger, rage, malice, slander, and filthy language
> from your mouth.
> (Colossians 3:8)

Anthony and Nina

Anthony and Nina are both volatile people. In disagreements they quickly move into belittling speech and painful verbal attacks, cursing and calling each other terrible names. They sound like a round of "Can you top this?"

Anthony usually "wins" the verbal barrage. Nina feels beaten down and hopeless. Emotionally and relationally bruised and battle worn, finally Anthony and Nina decide to limp into counseling.

They are calling a truce, committing to stop the attacks, learning different avenues of expressing emotions and solving differences. They realize that is the only solution for their marriage and opportunity for their hearts to begin to heal.

John and Cora

John and Cora have reached an impasse and need a neutral person to help their marriage. Cora regularly calls John names that disrespectfully mock him. He asks her to stop, but she says they are just nicknames.

Cora ignores how her name calling hurts John. She doesn't like to address the issue and thinks John should just accept it, saying, "It is no big deal." She gets very defensive and angry if anyone says anything negative toward her. Cora has a double standard and is dishonoring to John.

DISHONESTY

Lying, deception, and dishonesty break the trust in marriage. Lying is saying untrue things. Dishonesty and deception include misrepresenting and avoiding the truth because something wrong is being hidden. It is a plan to distract, detour, or detain from the truth being revealed.

Lying destroys the confidence and trustworthiness in the relationship. A pattern of lying can be to hide indicting things. It not only breaks the reliability in one area or one incident but is pervasive and harms the confidence of the relationship overall.

Trust is broken easily, but it takes a long time to restore it. Often there is a nonchalant attitude, as in "It wasn't that bad" or "You just need to trust me." Broken trust is devastating. The key to being trusted is to be trustworthy.

> A false witness will not go unpunished, and he who pours out lies will perish.
>
> (Proverbs 19:9)
>
> Do not lie to each other, since you have taken off your old self with its practices.
>
> (Colossians 3:9)

Leonard and Ruthie

Leonard and Ruthie are trying to rescue their marriage. Leonard has a history of lying. Recently, Ruthie found porn tracks and harmful websites on his computer. Devastated and angry, Ruthie sought help.

Leonard minimizes the deceitfulness and does not understand the demoralizing pain that it causes for Ruthie. However, it feels overwhelming to her, shatters her trust, and shows the marriage is broken. They need help to walk the path of restoration.

Rick and Elizabeth

Rick and Elizabeth are sorting out truth and lies in their marriage. Rick is finding misinformation as he investigates records. Elizabeth excessively shops online secretly and hides her scavenger spoils from Rick. She minimizes her deception and insatiable desires. Rick wants to trust her but feels discouraged and skeptical.

Elizabeth rationalizes her behaviors as she compares herself to others and wonders why Rick has to be so upset. She does not realize how her focus on material things has morphed into something bigger than her love and commitment to Rick and their marriage. Her destructive lying reveals heart issues also.

SARCASM AND CRUEL JOKING

Healthy, clean humor is positive and fun. However, sarcasm, cruel joking, and other painful forms of "humor" are harmful and sinful against others. Any form of negative communication that is labeled as joking or teasing is wrong.

No person deserves to be the brunt of any joke. People who express mean or cruel jokes relish the empowering control of inflicting pain and embarrassment on others. They would retaliate harshly if the same kind of sarcasm and joking came back on them.

These "jokers" minimize the sinful words with the lie, "I was only joking. Can't you take a joke?" The reality is that it is not joking. It is verbal and emotional abuse toward others and reveals a character flaw and sinful heart.

> Like a madman shooting firebrands or deadly
> arrows
> is a man who deceives his neighbor and says, "I
> was only joking!"
>
> (Proverbs 26:18-19)

> Nor should there be obscenity, foolish talk or
> coarse joking,
> which are out of place, but rather thanksgiving.
>
> (Ephesians 5:4)

> Put away perversity from your mouth;
> keep corrupt talk far from your lips.
>
> (Proverbs 4:24)

Albert and Alexia

Albert and Alexia are emotionally estranged. Alexia feels like from the time she wakes up to when she goes to bed at night, the relationship is filled with Albert's sarcasm and critical comments. He is constantly mocking Alexia and making her the object of his jokes.

Albert makes fun of Alexia's appearance, homemaking, ideas, opinions, feelings, and family. He laughs and can't understand why Alexia does not think it is funny. She feels so beaten down that she just wants to pull away from Albert and isolate herself from him.

INCONSISTENT COMMUNICATION

Stop and think before you speak. Words once spoken cannot be undone. Be intentional and careful with what you say. There should be kindness and consistency in our speaking. Everything spoken should be said in a respectful manner regardless of the circumstances or emotions.

Stop patterns of speaking nicely sometimes and then harshly at other times. God wants our heart and actions to be consistently loving. Going back and forth between thoughtful words and painful words shows double-mindedness. It reflects an unpredictable and untrustworthy person and shatters the confidence in the relationship.

> Out of the same mouth come praise and cursing.
> My brothers, this should not be.
>
> (James 3:10)

Denise and Larry

Denise feels hurt and disrespected in her marriage with Larry. He is nice sometimes and then at other times he is unkind and demeaning. She cannot trust his inconsistencies. Denise is emotionally shut down and guarded.

When things are going well, Larry is kind. When he is upset, he becomes very rude and critical. He becomes impatient, saying abrasive and hurtful things. Larry denies and minimizes it when Denise questions him about it.

Denise has decided to talk with her pastor. She feels so beaten down and disregarded. She is confused and discouraged. She needs encouragement and direction.

BROKEN PROMISES

Having a reputation of being a person of honor and integrity is priceless. Breaking promises is disappointing and disrespectful toward others. Following through on commitments builds reliability. It grants confidence to what was agreed. It is better not to make a commitment than to give one and not keep it.

Doing what we say we will do proves to others that our word is trustworthy and dependable. When a person commits to something and then does not follow through, it communicates that the person did not make it a priority and is not being accountable. That person does not treat others the way that he would like to be treated.

> A good name is more desirable than great riches;
> to be esteemed is better than silver or gold.
>
> (Proverbs 22:1)

> Simply let your "Yes" be "Yes," and your "No,"
> "No";
> anything beyond this comes from the evil one.
>
> (Matthew 5:37)

> Better a poor man whose walk is blameless than a fool whose lips are perverse.
>
> (Proverbs 19:1)

Gentry and Gloria

Gentry does not keep his word and often defaults on his commitments. Gloria has learned to doubt what he promises and wait to see if he follows through. The result is ambiguous trust in their marriage. For months Gentry has promised to fix some maintenance needs in their home, but he still has not bought the supplies or contacted people to hire who can help him.

When Gloria addresses it, Gentry renews his assurances without apologizing for past failures. He gets aggravated and defensive about his shortcomings with inconsiderate and deflective statements such as, "I'm just a terrible husband, and I can never do anything right." It sounds as if her expectations are the problem instead of his lack of follow through.

Gloria feels disappointed in the marriage even more than just the issue about repairs. She feels like Gentry has been unreliable in many areas of their marriage. She feels like she can't count on him and that he devalues the marriage.

Robert and Allison

Robert wants to encourage Allison but feels like she continues to break promises to him. He wonders if he can trust her. She has signed up several times to take classes at the local community college, hoping to try to finish her degree before they start a family.

Each time he pays the tuition; then she stops attending classes and doesn't turn in assignments without telling him. He is fine if she has changed her mind about finishing school, but he just wants her to be honest with him and keep commitments she makes. To him the trust in the relationship is more important than the degree.

All of these case studies reveal different ways that destructive communication can affect a marriage. It is crucial that harmful patterns be identified and that significant changes are made. There is so much at stake for the marriage to be healthy and give confident love to each spouse.

The hope for change is in knowing Jesus Christ as Savior and allowing Him to change your heart and habits. God loves you very much and has wonderful plans for you and your marriage. Seek Him and He will lead you.

> Therefore, if anyone is in Christ, he is a new creation; the old has gone, the new has come!
> (2 Corinthians 5:17)

SPECIFIC STEPS TO CHANGE DESTRUCTIVE COMMUNICATION

Identify your destructive communication habits. What have family members and others said about negative ways you interact? Pray about it. Ask some trusted people for input.

> If any of you lacks wisdom, he should ask God,
> who gives generously to all without finding fault,
> and it will be given to him.
>
> (James 1:5)

Confess your wrongdoing to family members and others when your conversations hurt others. Apologize to them.

> Therefore, confess your sins to each other and
> pray for each other so that you may be healed.
> The prayer of a righteous man is powerful and
> effective.
>
> (James 5:16)

Confess your sins to God. Let loved ones also hear your prayer and see your sincere remorse.

> If we confess our sins, he is faithful and just and
> will forgive us our sins and purify us from all
> unrighteousness.
>
> (1 John 1:9)

Stop destructive habits. Be accountable and willing to completely repent. Die to self, and love others more than yourself.

> I have been crucified with Christ and I no longer
> live, but Christ lives in me.
> The life I now live in the body, I live by faith in
> the Son of God,

who loved me and gave himself for me.

(Galatians 2:20)

Learn new, alternative ways to communicate. Replace the old patterns with new, respectful communication.

But now you must rid yourselves of all such things as these: anger, rage, malice, slander, and filthy language from your lips. Do not lie to each other since you have taken off your old self with its practices and have put on the new self, which is being renewed in knowledge in the image of its Creator.

(Colossians 3:8-10)

Enlist a godly mentor to help you be accountable. Thank your loved ones who are giving you the opportunity to stop destructive actions and begin new and better patterns. Commit to become a loving communicator. Select a mentor to encourage and guide you.

> As iron sharpens iron, so one man sharpens another.

(Proverbs 27:17)

> Trust God for the strength and help to change.
> I can do everything through Him who gives me strength.

(Philippians 4:13)

8

USEFUL TOOLS, TECHNIQUES, AND REMINDERS

> Set a guard over my mouth, O Lord;
> keep watch over the door of my lips.
>
> —Psalm 141:3

HAVING GOOD AND useful tools is essential in all areas of life to do the best job and enable the best success possible. In the same way, it is important in communication to have tools that can help couples and family members express what they want to say and understand each other better.

Useful tools encourage each person to make changes in the communication process, diverting negative aspects to positive methods. These enrich relationships and develop confidence and closeness. These tools, when implemented, will provide help to marriages and families.

REFLECTIVE LISTENING

Reflective listening is a listening skill. It is a method of increasing listening ability for connecting with the other person. Reflective listening is not about giving responses or opinions. It is not about evaluating or interpreting. It is about listening carefully to what is said.

Reflective listening may sound familiar as a communication technique. I would like to make changes and additions so that it is more productive and helpful. Reflective listening at first may seem cumbersome, but the effort, done respectfully, is worth it.

When you begin to use it correctly, you can see the benefits. It is good for couples to learn and practice reflective listening in normal conversations so they can know how to pivot to it easily when needed in stressful or conflicted conversations.

Reflective listening is similar to driving down a curvy mountain road and down shifting so the brakes don't get burned out and to avoid an accident. The goal of reflective listening is to slow the conversation so that emotions stay under control and no one gets hurt.

In the same way, it is important in conversations and especially in times of conflict to manage the intensity of the discussion so that words and emotions are appropriate. Avoiding misunderstandings is better than making mistakes, having regrets, and trying to correct things later.

Process

With reflective listening, the first person speaks and the second one listens for each major point. The speaker says three or four sentences and then stops. Then the speaker asks the listener to reflect, stating back the points of what was heard. Taking time to restate until each point is correctly reflected provides clarity and continuity.

It is easier to reflect as you go along instead of trying to catch up everything at the end. After every three or four sentences, the listener can invite more information by asking the speaker, "What else do you want to add?" "Tell me more."

The speaker continues several sentences at a time, stopping at the end to ask the listener to reflect and track together. The listener reflects the points after every few sentences. The listener waits until the speaker has stated the major points before switching places.

The responses will be different after listening to several sections of information instead of changing positions after each one. After a speaker has discussed several things, then that person may say, "That's enough for right now. Let's switch roles."

When the speaker and listener switch, it does not mean that is all the speaker wants to say. However, it will provide a good start. Each person can share several sections of facts and feelings. Then the couple can continue to work through the conversation more informed, attentive, and with increased understanding.

Additional Instructions

If you are the listener, and your spouse says something

that makes you want to respond, correct, interrupt, or add to, write a word or two to remind you of that point. That will help you pay attention, but not forget your thoughts. Avoid interrupting.

Patiently allow your spouse to express several sections of thoughts and feelings before you become the speaker. That gives you valuable information and will give honor to your spouse. Then as the speaker, express your opinions and feelings. Allow your spouse to reflect back.

Benefits

In normal communication one may wonder if the other person is listening and hearing what is being said. With little response from the listener, a speaker may doubt the listener is paying attention.

That is why someone speaking may state the instruction or content repeatedly. Reflection shows that the other person is hearing what is said. Then move to the next point.

For instance, a mother of a teenager may repeat instructions while the teenager is distracted by something else and is not obeying. Slow down and state clearly. Ask the teenager to reflect the instructions. Then accountability will be in the obedience.

VALIDATION CHART

VALIDATION CHART

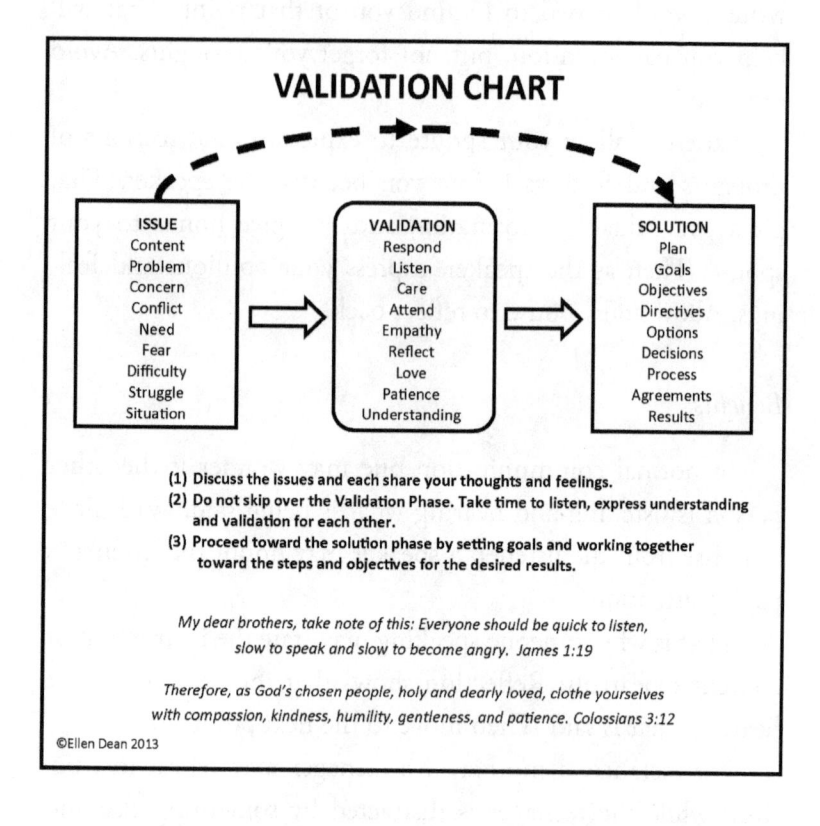

ISSUE	VALIDATION	SOLUTION
Content	Respond	Plan
Problem	Listen	Goals
Concern	Care	Objectives
Conflict	Attend	Directives
Need	Empathy	Options
Fear	Reflect	Decisions
Difficulty	Love	Process
Struggle	Patience	Agreements
Situation	Understanding	Results

(1) Discuss the issues and each share your thoughts and feelings.
(2) Do not skip over the Validation Phase. Take time to listen, express understanding and validation for each other.
(3) Proceed toward the solution phase by setting goals and working together toward the steps and objectives for the desired results.

My dear brothers, take note of this: Everyone should be quick to listen, slow to speak and slow to become angry. James 1:19

Therefore, as God's chosen people, holy and dearly loved, clothe yourselves with compassion, kindness, humility, gentleness, and patience. Colossians 3:12

©Ellen Dean 2013

The validation chart is a tool I developed to help people pause to care about the other person's feelings and perspectives. It is designed to increase understanding, express emotions, develop empathy, and provide feelings of being understood and valued.

It also offers a careful progression of addressing what the issues are, acknowledging emotions, and then moving toward problem solving and positive actions. Common clichés for wives are, "I just want my husband to listen." And for husbands to say, "I want to be able to fix things." However, these alone are incomplete.

Both of these elements are important in marriage and other relationships. The key is the appropriate balance. The relationship needs to experience a sense of validating emotions and also seeking practical solutions. A relationship can feel distant and uncaring without meaningful understanding of emotions and can feel stuck without movement toward constructive goals.

The Validation Chart helps communication participants learn to identify the issues and focus on content. It helps to bring discussion about the emotions with understanding toward one another. Then it explores goals and productive action plans.

The natural tendencies of husbands and wives to lean toward the emotional or the logical is part of what makes marriage wonderful. Yet when the marriage reaches a stalemate, it can feel debilitating. Appropriate and adequate flow confirms emotions and takes positive steps.

If a wife thinks her husband does not care about her feelings, she feels alone and devalued. When a husband thinks he can never take actions and solve problems, he feels powerless and immobilized. Working to improve both is the best outcome.

On the Validation Chart the first section is a cluster of synonyms for issues and topics that a marriage may need to discuss. It is important to identify pertinent subjects to discuss. Often it will encompass more than one topic.

There is usually a plethora of different emotions that spouses feel attached to specific topics and issues. It is crucial for couples to identify and share their feelings and viewpoints. Honor one another by recognizing your spouse's emotions and giving them validity.

It takes time and attention to offer comfort and kindness toward a spouse when feelings are flooding over, especially when you may not have the same feelings. Pausing to recognize all the emotions in situations lovingly values your spouse and helps your marriage grow in trust.

Spending time discussing feelings is important. However, when a spouse hopes to linger a long time just receiving the compassion of the other spouse, it may become too limiting. There must also be a willingness to move toward solutions and positive outcomes.

Move into the objectives phase by setting goals and working together toward a plan for the desired positive results. This honors the spouse who is feeling the urgency to make progress toward growth and solutions.

Ronnie and Claire

Ronnie had just bought Claire a new car and she was so excited. In just a few days she was in a car accident. Claire was not hurt, but her new car was damaged. That night as they discussed it, Ronnie was saying, "I'm glad you are okay. We'll get your car fixed." Ronnie didn't understand why Claire kept crying.

Finally, she was able to put into words that she wanted him to understand her feelings as well as discuss plans to fix the car. Sympathizing with her about the disappointment and sadness of the car accident can go together with the hope and good news of repairing the car. Both are important.

Claire needs to be willing to move toward the positive stage of choosing a thankful attitude in spite of the circumstances. Allowing Ronnie to guide her to look toward hope and a positive outcome is good for her. It also encourages Ronnie emotionally.

REGULATORS AND TIMERS

Some helpful tools in communication include ways of establishing equity and fairness in dividing the time for sharing by each spouse. Otherwise, one spouse can be more verbal and dominate the time, intensity, content, and outcome.

Regulators such as timers and alarms help keep the conversation moving so there is beneficial input from both spouses for the most positive results. The goal of communication is to discuss and process topics, feelings, and experiences.

Early in my counseling I had small samples of linoleum floor covering. I would use these as visual reminders of "You take the floor" or "Now you have the floor" so the couple could take turns talking. Holding an item can identify who is talking and who is listening.

Setting an agreed time frame allows both spouses to share personal thoughts and feelings in a fair way. A timer is objective. Generally, one to two minutes of talking allows for a good amount of information to be discussed. Then switch to the other person.

Amounts of time usually seem less when we are personally talking. Listening to someone else feels longer. That is what makes it easy to lose track of time when we are speaking. A neutral measuring device helps. Set the timer on your phone and let it be the arbitrative guide.

Agree together for the method and amount of time for each speaking turn. Respect your spouse by keeping the agreement. When it is your turn, avoid the temptation of saying, "Just one more thing" or "Let me just finish this," and yet really extend it more. Kindly wrap up your turn quickly when your time is up.

EFFECTIVE USE OF QUESTIONS

Effective questions are an important tool to help communication stay on track. They also open up additional areas of exploring content and emotions. Pertinent and timely questions can solicit more information and encourage input.

Questions to Invite More Information

Some of these questions may include: "What are your thoughts about this topic?" "What are your feelings?" "What do you want for yourself?" "What do you want for me?" "What do you want for us?" "How can I act in your interest?" "What are the problems and concerns?" "What are the solutions?"

Questions to Clarify

Some of these questions may include: "What would you say are the main issues?" "Did you get to say all you wanted to say?" "Any additional thoughts or feelings you want to share?" "What do you think my preferences are?" "What steps do you want us to take?" "What are the most important things to you regarding this?" "What can I do to help you?" "How can I show you I love you?" "How can I serve you?

IMPORTANT REMINDERS

A Word to Husbands

Often some of the most dreaded words a husband can hear from a wife are "We need to talk" or "There is something I would like talk about." Please do not assume the worst about these statements.

Typically, these words are not to strike fear into the heart of the husband, not to play "gotcha" or to imply that the husband is "in trouble." Rather, they generally show that the wife is wanting to address an issue so the marriage can be strengthened and improved.

Wives are often more detail-oriented about specific growth areas in the marriage. A wife cares deeply about the marriage. She may feel that it is good overall but wants to address some minor specific issues. Think of it as a way the wife is saying that the marriage is very valuable and investing in it is important. She cares deeply about it.

The husband may be tempted to think that he can never measure up or get it all right, even when the wife may not think the husband has done poorly. It is tempting to make comments of resignation or futility that are not true. Do not make statements to rationalize your lack of commitment or willingness to change. Be the best you can be in the marriage.

Yes, you can measure up and get it right. Be willing to put forth the effort without throwing in the towel so quickly. Most often that statement is not a reflection of the wife's critical attitude, but rather of the lack of emotional desire on the part of the husband. It indicates relational laziness. Step up and care about your marriage as much as your wife does.

A Word to Wives

Be considerate of your husband by giving him a "heads-up" about issues you want to discuss so he does not feel blindsided. Do not try to catch him off guard or put him on the spot. Be respectful of the timing for important discussions.

Remember, it takes emotional energy to resolve issues. Try to find times when you both have sufficient physical and mental reserve to discuss together, process adequately, and come to a shared conclusion. Allow for equal sharing and listening.

Begin the conversation with praise and affirmation for good things he does. Let him know that you appreciate him. That will help to alleviate concerns or defensiveness. Express your love for him and your desires for the marriage to be great.

Share your concerns or ideas. Avoid extreme statements. Talk through things calmly with your husband. Do not come with your mind made up or determined that things can only be your way. Take time to really glean from your husband's wisdom and ideas. Have an open mind for compromise.

Healthy marriages work together, respectful of each other's perspectives and emotions. Communication is the channel for relational growth and strength. Make sure dialogue is positive and open to bring greater heart connection.

Do Not Give Up on Good Communication; Do Not Give in to Bad Communication

When met with loudness and emotional intensity from the spouse, continue to talk calmly—not in a self-righteous, patronizing way but in a genuine, kind way that will invite the other person to calm down. Say, "I do not want us to hurt each other with our words."

If the other person is out of control, in sinful anger, or refusing to listen, calmly say, "I want to talk with you about this, but our conversation now is not good. When we can talk calmly and in a controlled and respectful way, I am available to talk together." Then disengage until emotions and methods can be reset more productively.

When someone is not letting you speak, ask for a chance to respond. If not, call for a break. Set a parameter. Then try again. If the intensity is still high, delay the discussion till it can be calm and respectful. You may need to consider bringing in a third objective person. Your thoughts are important too and deserve to be heard. (See Chapter "Connecting in Conflicts.")

Do not make assumptions about others or let others make assumptions about you. Request that each person speak about his or her own emotions and opinions. Do not say what you think the other is thinking or feeling. Listen to your spouse's information. Each should put accurate personal thoughts and feelings into words.

Provide relational energy to pursue and move toward the relationship. Each spouse should make the marriage the priority it deserves to be. Show that you care. Engage. Ask questions allowing the other person to share his or her perspectives. Then share yours.

Do not have so much confidence in your own position that you fail to listen to the other person. Whether this is your spouse or your child, they are worth listening to, and their thoughts are equally valuable as yours. Even expressing that to them is very loving.

Checklist for Crisis Management

Identify issues; write down bullet points to discuss. Discuss concisely. Lower emotions and volume; talk through issues one at a time; develop a plan; and follow through.

Take time-outs as needed. State guidelines to define them. Follow up to resume discussion.

Agree on scriptures that provide guidance for positive, respectful communication.

Bring in an objective third person when needed.

SUMMARIES AND EVALUATIONS

Summarize conversations to solidify main points and agreements.

Debrief together for future improvement. Evaluate communication methods and patterns. Stay open to suggestions. Discuss some needed growth methods and future commitments.

Positive relationships are gifts from God. They deserve to be treated carefully with grace and kindness. Treasure them. Grow to be a more loving and respectful communicator.

Choose to love God and honor others in all your words and actions. When Jesus was asked what was the most important commandment, He responded with the following.

> "The most important one," answered Jesus, "is this:
> 'Hear, O Israel: the Lord our God, the Lord is one.
> Love the Lord your God with all your heart and with all your soul and with all your mind and

with all your strength.'
The second is this: 'Love your neighbor as yourself.'
There is no commandment greater than these."

(Mark 12:29-31)

9

FREQUENTLY ASKED QUESTIONS ABOUT COMMUNICATION

> Let your conversation be always full of grace, seasoned with salt,
> so that you may know how to answer everyone.
> —Colossians 4:6

WHAT IF I CAN'T THINK OF ANYTHING TO SAY?

IT IS COMMON to hear, "I just can't say what I want to say," "I have trouble putting my thoughts and feelings into words," "I have to think about my words carefully," "I can't communicate like I wish I could."

The good news is that everyone who wants to become a better communicator can become one. Often the debilitating feelings may result from a lack of guidance in communication or possibly hurtful past experiences. It may also stem from a preoccupation with self and the fear of what others will think.

Shifting the focus from self to interest in others will distract from personal fearfulness. Have a genuine desire to get to know other people. Seek to gather information from others to learn about their interests and desires. Ask questions about them and be interested in their responses.

Ask questions in a respectful way. Talk to people in the way that you would want others to communicate with you. Don't worry so much about what you are going to say, but more about what is positive and caring to others.

WHAT IF MY SPOUSE IS ANTAGONISTIC IN COMMUNICATION?

God does not want marriage partners to be contentious or antagonistic toward each other. If your spouse is disrespectful or adversarial, address that with your spouse. Express that you want your marriage to be harmonious and unified. If you need to have someone present to help talk with your spouse, find a trusted family member or friend to help you.

There should be immediate and consistent improvement. Aggression in marriage sets up a conflicted relationship which is very harmful. Spouses should be united and on the same team, not enemies. If that is not the situation, seek an objective person to help recalibrate the marriage to be positive again. You may need someone to advocate for you.

WHAT IF MY SPOUSE JUST WON'T TALK?

If a spouse will not talk, ask what the feelings and hesitancies might be. Be attentive and caring. Sometimes the reasons might range from relationship disinterest, distractions, personal laziness, or oppression from past or present relationships.

Ask questions to understand so the marriage can be enriched. If there is not improvement and answers don't explain the problems, then consider seeking professional or ministerial help. Whatever the reasons are, it is difficult to have the special communication and emotional closeness your marriage deserves without your spouse being willing to meaningfully contribute to conversations.

WHAT IF MY SPOUSE GOES ON AND ON?

If your spouse has a tendency to talk for lengthy periods of time, discuss it together to understand the reasons for that. Perhaps your spouse is unaware but is willing to change and learn to set good boundaries.

However, if your spouse denies it, responds with a lack of concern, or becomes angry about the "accusation," pause the conversation. Ask your spouse to consider your concerns, become more aware of the detrimental patterns, and be willing to change.

Talk with your spouse about having the freedom to bring it to his or her attention when this is occurring in conversations. Perhaps you and your spouse can develop a signal for those times when he or she is rambling or repeating.

If your spouse is going on and on in conversations with you, ask her to be more concise and succinct in what she says.

Let her know that you care about what she wants to say and that you will listen. Pay attention so she will not feel the need to keep repeating.

If you notice that your spouse is talking excessively when in conversation with others, perhaps you can discreetly let him know that is happening. Offer suggestions on how to help him express things efficiently and concisely.

If more help is needed, seek outside advice and counsel from a counselor or minister who can help you talk with your spouse. Discuss the feelings of being run over and marginalized.

WHAT IF MY SPOUSE IS NEGATIVE AND CRITICAL?

If your spouse is negative and critical, discuss it with your spouse. Sometimes bad patterns become habits and creep in without the other person being aware of it. Hopefully, your spouse will be apologetic and remorseful, committing to be different.

However, if your spouse is angry about the discussion, denies it, blames you, or responds with more disrespect, seek help from an outsider. Your spouse is using some verbal and emotional abuse to be oppressive, and it needs to be addressed and corrected. Bad communication is not a reflection of the listener, but rather the speaker.

Do not assume all the responsibility personally. Do not try to change things alone unless there is a genuine willingness to change by your spouse. Do not allow yourself to be pulled into increased anger and nonproductive conversations.

WHAT IF MY SPOUSE IS UNTRUTHFUL?

If your spouse is untruthful or dishonest, it is important that you address that. Trust is foundational to a healthy marriage, and the trust is broken every time there is any untruthfulness. Your spouse should be willing to acknowledge and confess the untruthfulness, apologize, and be fully transparent with the truth and facts.

Do not think you have to keep this a secret. Confide in a trusted, helpful person as needed. If the pattern persists or if there is denial and a lack of full honest disclosure, seek outside help from a minister or counselor. People lie and are dishonest because they do not want the truth exposed. They are usually hiding something. Honesty welcomes transparency and accountability.

Habitual lying and dishonesty can be a characteristic of some severe emotional and mental disorders. Seek professional help if needed. It can also be a clear heart picture and reveal a concerning spiritual condition.

WHAT IF MY FAMILY HAD A LOT OF ANGER AND SO DO I?

Families do influence patterns and habits. Communication and how emotions are processed and expressed positively and negatively can be internalized by observing others in families. Individuals should evaluate how their family of origin has influenced them.

Determine to incorporate the good and lay aside the less desirable patterns. Do not imagine that you have to be angry because you grew up in an angry family. In fact, it is your responsibility to address wrong, angry behavior and commit to be different.

The good news is that we are not powerless to duplicate our family of origin or any negative pattern that has been modeled for us. Each person can choose to handle things in positive and right ways. In fact, no adult has any excuse to say, "That was how my family did it" to explain their own bad behavior.

Practice the good decisions and behaviors you want to include in your life. Treat people with respect. Replace your sinful anger with appropriate ways of handling emotions. Choose to be gentle and loving in all your communications.

> When I was a child, I talked like a child, I thought like a child,
> I reasoned like a child. When I became a man,
> I put childish ways behind me.
>
> (1 Corinthians 13:11)

CAN I LEARN TO COMMUNICATE BETTER?

Yes, the good news is that anyone can learn to become a better communicator. Being a good communicator involves having a genuine interest in other people, a desire to treat all people with consideration and respect, and a willingness to apply good communication skills.

Basic communication practices include using appropriate positive and clean words, listening to others, respectful flow of dialogue, appreciating others, responding kindly, and engaging with positive interests and information.

WHAT IF I SAY THE WRONG THING?

Communication is not so much about saying "the right things." There are not certain words to say. It is more about saying appropriate things based on thoughtfulness and respect for others. If you accidentally say the wrong thing, apologize to the other participants. Be genuine in your remorse and commit to correcting the mistakes.

However, if something is said that is not honest, considerate, or appropriate, immediate response is needed. There should be humble acknowledgment, confession, apology, and corrections back to what is accurate, positive, and loving.

HOW SHOULD I EXPRESS FRUSTRATIONS OR CONCERNS?

This really depends on what the frustrations and concerns are and to whom you want to express them. Generally, the best guidelines are to approach any person with any concern in a calm and considerate way. Be honest about your feelings and thoughts.

Go directly to the person involved if possible. Involve others if necessary, but still discuss in an appropriate way. Address specific issues in gentle and respectful methods. Seek what is right and good. Discuss concerns in ways that are clear and positive. Choose to adhere to right guidelines for best outcomes.

WHAT IF MY SPOUSE TALKS NEGATIVELY ABOUT ME TO OTHERS?

If your spouse talks negatively about you to others, address the issues with your spouse. If you hear it directly or from other people, ask your spouse about it. It may be helpful to include the person from whom you heard about the negative comments.

Ask your spouse about the facts. Then explain how it hurts your feelings and harms the relationship. Discuss that it breaks your trust, feels disrespectful, and causes problems in the marriage. It makes you want to pull away and not be close.

Hopefully, your spouse will be very responsive and remorseful. Discuss guidelines about the importance of talking about each other in loving and kindhearted ways to each other and to others in all circumstances. If you need someone to support you in this conversation, enlist that person to help you.

HOW CAN WE SLOW COMMUNICATION DOWN?

Pacing communication in appropriate ways is important. Conversations are positive when the speed is good for the participants to be able to contribute. Discussions can become one-sided if there is excessive commentary on one side or if one participant talks so fast that no one else can enter the conversation.

During intense conversations, the exchange can escalate quickly and soon the participants are talking fast, talking over each other, and not listening to each other. This type of conversation is fruitless and alienates the participants.

A time-out may need to be called with clear parameters and time frames before returning to the discussion. The time-out is designed to slow down the conversation and lower the intensity. Reflective listening (Useful Tools and Techniques chapter) is also a good tool to slow down conversations.

10

THE MOST AMAZING COMMUNICATION

The heavens declare the glory of God;
the skies proclaim the work of his hands.
Day after day they pour forth speech;
night after night they display knowledge.
There is no speech or language
where their voice is not heard.
Their voice goes out into all the earth,
their words to the ends of the world.
In the heavens he has pitched a tent for the sun,
which is like a bridegroom coming forth from his pavilion,
like a champion rejoicing to run his course.
It rises at one end of the heavens

and makes its circuit to the other;
nothing is hidden from its heat.

—Psalm 19:1-6

GOD IS A Communicator. God communicates with us. These statements seem simple and maybe even a matter of fact. However, they are absolutely profound. Our minds cannot even begin to understand the depth of the fact that Almighty God of the Universe actively communicates with each person, but it is true.

Recently, I was driving to work one morning and saw a glorious heavenly sight. All over the sky above me were extremely dark, thick clouds as if a strong storm was coming soon. Then suddenly from a break in the clouds shone the most amazing sparkling burst of sunrise rays that I can ever remember. It was just a speck of the glorious magnificence of God's creation.

In a few minutes the sky changed again, and the morning brightened into lighter blues and grays. I wondered how many people driving on that interstate highway that morning sensed and felt a reminder of the splendor and unlimited awesomeness of God.

Psalm 19 teaches that the heavens declare the magnificent glory of the Lord and the skies proclaim the work of His hands. Day after day they pour forth speech, and night after night they display knowledge. Their voice goes out into all the earth, and their words to the end of the world.

We can almost imagine a glorious orchestra playing in the background as the crescendo builds with the colorful canopy of the skies. The heavens declare that God has pitched a tent for the sun, which is like a bridegroom coming forth from his pavilion, like a champion rejoicing to run his course. It rises at one of the heavens and makes its circuit to the other; nothing is hidden from its heat. The fabulous creation of our Lord is breathtaking and calls forth from us a chorus of praise and exaltation.

What do the heavens proclaim? They announce God's creativity, grandeur, power, love, and order in the universe. He allows us to look up into the sky and see the daily changes and powerful movement of His sun, moon, stars, clouds, sunrises, and sunsets.

He lets us see the peaceful beauty of the skies at times and the dramatic weather changes that can form at other times. We are reminded that only God can control the heavens, earth, and His universe. He created this world to provide sustenance for mankind and give us what we need for our physical existence.

All people can look into the heavens, see nature, and believe that there is a God who has created the world and everything in it. They can be in awe of God's creation and His sustaining control, protections, and provisions on this earth.

However, nature alone cannot explain that God's love sent His precious Son, Jesus Christ, to earth for us. Jesus Christ, who is God, came to earth to die for the sins of mankind and to offer salvation to all people, who will receive Him (John 1:12).

Jesus Christ promises forgiveness for sins and eternal life with Him in Heaven. That is why we must proclaim about Jesus Christ to this lost and broken world. We need to communicate clearly the truth of the Gospel.

Jesus came, died on the cross, and rose again to bring redemption and forgiveness to all who will trust in Him. Everyone needs to know the truth about Jesus Christ in order to accept Him as their personal Savior.

> The law of the LORD is perfect,
> reviving the soul.
> The statutes of the LORD are trustworthy,
> making wise the simple.
> The precepts of the LORD are right,
> giving joy to the heart.
> The commands of the LORD are radiant,
> giving light to the eyes.
> The fear of the LORD is pure,
> enduring forever.
> The ordinances of the LORD are sure
> and altogether righteous.
> They are more precious than gold,
> than much pure gold;
> they are sweeter than honey,
> than honey from the comb.
> By them is your servant warned;
> in keeping them there is great reward.
>
> (Psalm 19:7-11)

This passage teaches about the importance of God's Word, the Bible. The Bible is called the Word of God because it is God communicating to us. The Bible is "God breathed" (2 Timothy 3:16). God's Holy Spirit directed the writing of the Bible. It is God's divinely inspired guidebook to this world. It is another powerful way that God speaks to us.

Psalm 19 helps us understand that the Bible is filled with God's laws, statutes, precepts, and commands which "are more precious than gold." The person who obeys them will receive a great reward. God has carefully communicated His word to us and has promised that it will bless and help our life when we read and obey it.

God knows that we desperately need Him and His guidance in our lives. The Bible gives wisdom and understanding to know how to have a personal relationship with Jesus Christ. It gives instructions for how to live life, relate to other people, and make decisions. The Bible guides us in how to communicate in ways that strengthen and benefit our meaningful relationships.

> Who can discern his errors?
> Forgive my hidden faults.
> Keep your servant also from willful sins;
> may they not rule over me.
> Then will I be blameless,
> innocent of great transgression.
> May the words of my mouth and the meditation
> of my heart
> be pleasing in your sight,
> O Lord, my Rock and my Redeemer.
>
> (Psalm 19:12-14)

In verse 14 of Psalm 19, King David prays that he wants the words of his mouth and the meditations of his heart to be acceptable to God. We also should want our thoughts and words to honor God and please Him. That is why learning to communicate in a good and effective way is honoring to God and kind to others. The Bible helps us to live for God.

GOD'S MOST IMPORTANT COMMUNICATION — THE WORD BECAME FLESH

In the beginning was the Word, and the Word was

with God, and the Word was God.
He was with God in the beginning. Through him
all things were made;
without him nothing was made that has been
made. In him was life,
and that life was the light of men. The light shines
in the darkness,
but the darkness has not understood it.

(John 1:1-5)

This passage states that Jesus Christ, the Word, was with God before the world began. It also says that Jesus Christ was God. The Word, Jesus Christ, became flesh and dwelt among us. Jesus is the eternal Word. The most meaningful communication this world has ever known or will ever know was when God sent His Son, Jesus Christ, to the earth.

This amazing message of love and grace is life-changing for every person who believes and receives Christ personally. God broke through all time and history to come to the earth to be born as a tiny baby, in a humble barn and lying in a manger.

He came with one purpose: to live the perfect life, to die on the cross to pay for the sins of mankind and then to resurrect to give eternal life. In dying on the rugged cross, He offered forgiveness for our sins. We could never pay the price for our sins ourselves. They require a perfect and holy sacrifice.

Only God Himself, Jesus Christ, could be that exclusive sacrifice for our sins. He died for us, so that by believing in Him, trusting in His death and His resurrection, we can receive forgiveness for our sins and salvation. With that, we also receive the Holy Spirit to abide in us, abundant life now, and eternal life in Heaven.

> The true light that gives light to every man was
> coming into the world.
> He was in the world, and though the world was
> made through him,
> the world did not recognize him. He came to that
> which was his own,
> but his own did not receive him. Yet to all who
> received him,
> to those who believed in his name,
> he gave the right to become children of God—
> children born not of natural descent, nor of hu-
> man decision or a husband's will,
> but born of God. The Word became flesh and
> made his dwelling among us.
> We have seen his glory, the glory of the One and
> Only,
> who came from the Father, full of grace and truth.
>
> (John 1:9-14)

Everyone needs to hear that people are lost and separated from God because of sin. We must recognize our sinfulness. We must understand that every person needs a Savior to pay the price for sins. We can do nothing to pay for our own sins. Without Jesus Christ, we would face the punishment for our sinfulness, which is eternal death. We need a Savior to rescue us from eternal death and punishment, which is Hell.

Jesus Christ is that Savior! He who is perfect came to earth in human form to be the substitute to die for our sins. Christ willingly died on the cross to pay the penalty for our sins and to provide a way of salvation for us and to each person who trusts in Him.

In order to receive the salvation that God offers to us, each person must recognize that he or she is a sinner and needs forgiveness from God. Believe that Jesus Christ died on the cross to offer forgiveness for our sins.

Every person must pray, asking Jesus to forgive his or her sins and to be their Savior and Lord. This is a decision to live for God for all our life, seeking to honor and obey Him in all things. It is the most important decision anyone will ever make. When a person makes this crucial decision, he or she can have confidence of eternal life in Heaven after death.

Jesus Christ alone gives abundant life now with true meaning, purpose, and joy in life. He also promises eternal life with God for all those who believe in Him.

CPSIA information can be obtained
at www.ICGtesting.com
Printed in the USA
FSHW021536051020